Liberia

Libya

Liechtenstein
Lithuania
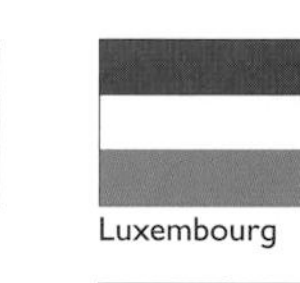
Luxembourg

Macedonia, FYRO
Madagascar

Malawi

Malaysia
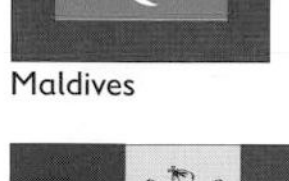
Maldives
Mali

Malta

Marshall Islands

Mauritania

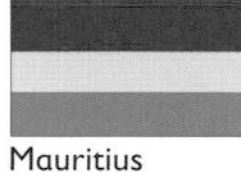
Mauritius

Mexico

Moldova
Monaco

Mongolia
Montenegro

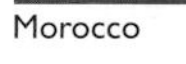
Morocco

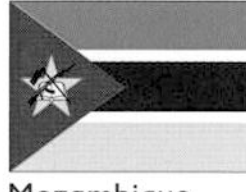
Mozambique

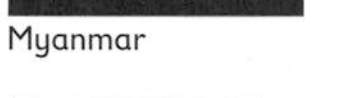
Myanmar

Namibia
Nauru

Nepal
Netherlands

New Zealand

Nicaragua
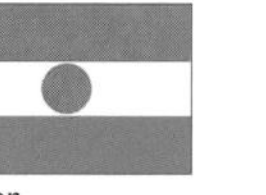
Niger
Nigeria

North Korea

Norway
Oman
Pakistan

Palau

Panama
Papua New Guinea

Paraguay

Peru
Philippines
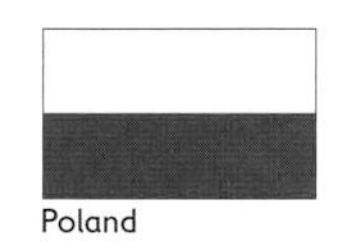
Poland

Portugal

Qatar
Romania
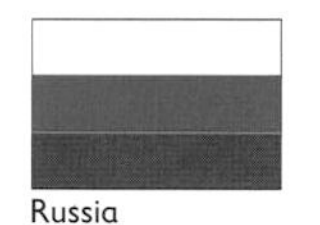
Russia

Rwanda
St. Kitts and Nevis

St. Lucia

St.Vincent & the Grenadines
Samoa
San Marino
Sao Tomé and Pirncipe

Saudi Arabia

Senegal
Serbia

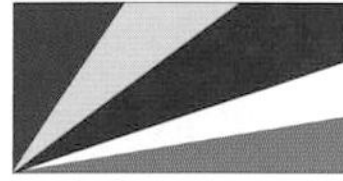
Seychelles

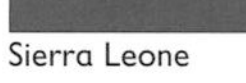
Sierra Leone
Singapore

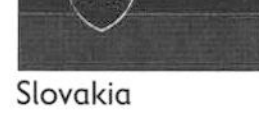
Slovakia

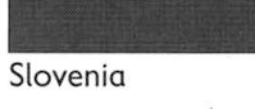
Slovenia
Solomon Islands
Somalia

South Africa
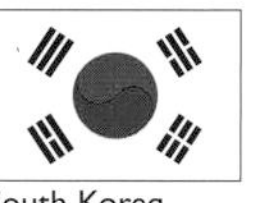
South Korea
South Sudan
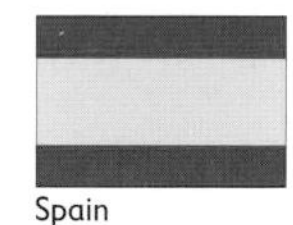
Spain

Sri Lanka
Sudan
Suriname

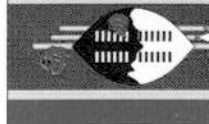
Swaziland

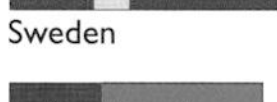
Sweden
Switzerland

Syria

Taiwan
Tajikistan
Tanzania

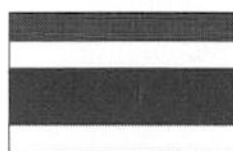
Thailand

Togo
Tonga

Trinidad and Tobago

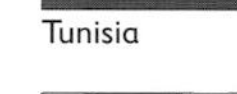
Tunisia
Turkey
Turkmenistan

Tuvalu

Uganda

Ukraine
United Arab Emirates

United Kingdom
United States of America
Uruguay

Uzbekistan

Vanuatu
Venezuela

Vietnam
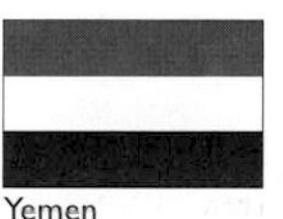
Yemen
Zambia
Zimbabwe

Oxford First Atlas

Editorial Adviser
Dr Patrick Wiegand

OXFORD
UNIVERSITY PRESS

Great Clarendon Street, Oxford OX2 6DP

Oxford University Press is a department of the University of Oxford.
It furthers the University's objective of excellence in research, scholarship,
and education by publishing worldwide in

Oxford New York

Auckland Cape Town Dar es Salaam Hong Kong Karachi
Kuala Lumpur Madrid Melbourne Mexico City Nairobi
New Delhi Shanghai Taipei Toronto

With offices in

Argentina Austria Brazil Chile Czech Republic France Greece
Guatemala Hungary Italy Japan Poland Portugal Singapore
South Korea Switzerland Thailand Turkey Ukraine Vietnam

Oxford is a registered trade mark of Oxford University Press
in the UK and in certain other countries

First published 2010

ISBN 978 0 19 848785 2 (hardback)
ISBN 978 0 19 848784 5 (paperback)

13 15 17 19 20 18 16 14 12

Printed in Singapore by KHL Printing Co. Pte Ltd.

Paper used in the production of this book is a natural, recyclable product made from wood grown in sustainable forests.
The manufacturing process conforms to the environmental regulations of the country of origin.

Acknowledgements

The publishers would like to thank the following for permission to reproduce photographs:

3a Planetary Visions Ltd/Science Photo Library, 4a Planet Observer/Science Photo Library, 8a David Lyons/Alamy, 8b Design Pics Inc/Rex Features, 8c John Warburton-Lee/Photolibrary.com, 8d Christopher Elwell/Shutterstock.com, 10a Gary Brown/Rex Features, 10b Arco Images GmbH/Alamy, 10c Micha Pawlitzki/Corbis, 10d Des Willie/Alamy, 10e SGM SGM/Photolibrary.com, 12a Alan Copson/Photolibrary.com, 12b OUP/Corel, 12c Simon Batley/Alamy, 12d Geoff A Howard/Alamy, 13a Alinari/Rex Features, 16a John Frumm/Photolibrary.com, 16b Sue Flood/Getty Images, 16c John Henry Claude Wilson/ Photolibrary.com, 17a Alexandra Winkler/Reuters/Corbis, 18a Leonid Shcheglov/Shutterstock.com, 18b Joe Fox/Alamy,18c Charles Stirling/Alamy, 18d Britain on View/Photolibrary.com, 18e OUP/Corel, 20a Arco Images GmbH/Alamy, 20b Marianna Sulic/Getty Images, 20c Hashim Pudiyapura/Shutterstock.com, 20d Paul Banton/Shutterstock.com, 21a Juan Carlos Munoz/Photolibrary.com, 21b Corbis/Photolibrary.com, 21c moodboard/Photolibrary.com, 22a Joe McDonald/Corbis, 22b Rafael Ramirez Lee/Shutterstock.com, 23a Jan Gottwald/Shutterstock.com, 23b OUP/Corbis, 24a Getmapping PLC/Science Photo Library, 26a Gavin Hellier/Getty Images, 26b Reuters/Corbis, 26c Sarah Leen/Getty Images, 27a Ted Mead/Photolibrary.com, 28a Chris Warren/Photolibrary of Wales, 28b Amra Pasic/Shutterstock.com, 28c Rex Butcher/Getty Images, 28d Ken McKay/Rex Features, 28e Phil Noble/Reuters/Corbis, 28f Rod Edwards/Photolibrary.com, 30a Feraru Nicolae/Shutterstock.com, 30b OUP/Corbis, 30c Wong Tsu Shi/Shutterstock.com, 30d Pborowka/Shutterstock.com, 31a Craig Hanson/Shutterstock.com, 31b TOSP Photo/Shutterstock.com, 35a Siepmann Siepmann/Photolibrary.com, 35b prism68/Shutterstock.com, 37a Rex/Rex Features, 37b Dahlquist Ron/Photolibrary.com, 39a Joshua Haviv/Shutterstock.com, 39b Graça Victoria/Shutterstock.com, 39c OUP/Photodisc, 39d Andre Jenny/Alamy, 41a JTB Photo Communications, Inc./Alamy, 41b Paul Souders/Getty Images, 41c Yoshio Tomii Photo Studio/Photolibrary.com, 41d Tom C Amon/Shutterstock.com, 43a Alan Ward/Shutterstock.com, 43b OUP/Digital Vision, 43c Neil Cooper/Alamy, 43d David C Poole/Photolibrary.com, 45a Purestock/Photolibrary.com, 45b OUP/Photodisc, 45c Jeff Hunter/Getty Images, 45d Steve Wisbauer/Getty Images, 46a Bryan & Cherry Alexander Photography/Alamy, 47a blickwinkel/Alamy

Illustrations by Mark Brierley

Cover illustrations by Galia Bernstein. Cover globe by Jan Rysavy/iStockphoto

Contents

The Earth is a planet in space. It is a sphere.

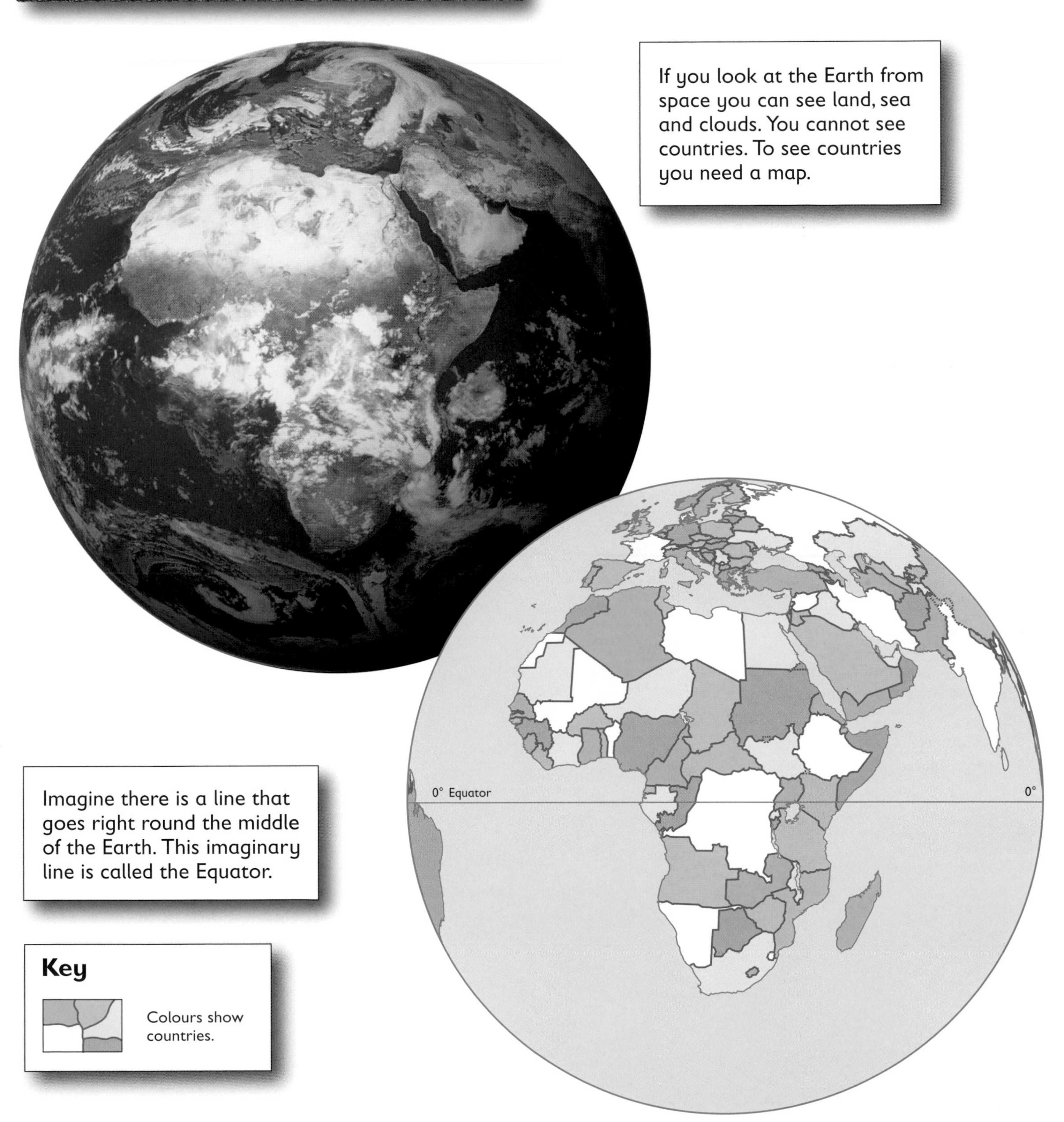

If you look at the Earth from space you can see land, sea and clouds. You cannot see countries. To see countries you need a map.

Imagine there is a line that goes right round the middle of the Earth. This imaginary line is called the Equator.

Key

Colours show countries.

Transverse Mercator Projection

4 The British Isles

Great Britain and Ireland are islands. They are land with sea all around. These two large islands, together with many smaller ones, make up the British Isles.

This is a picture of the British Isles from space.

This is a map of the British Isles.

There are two countries in the British Isles. The key shows what the colours and symbols on the map stand for.

Key

United Kingdom

Republic of Ireland

■ capital city

Dublin ■

Republic of Ireland

United Kingdom

London ■

The British Isles are small compared to many places in the world. Can you find the British Isles on a globe?

The United Kingdom

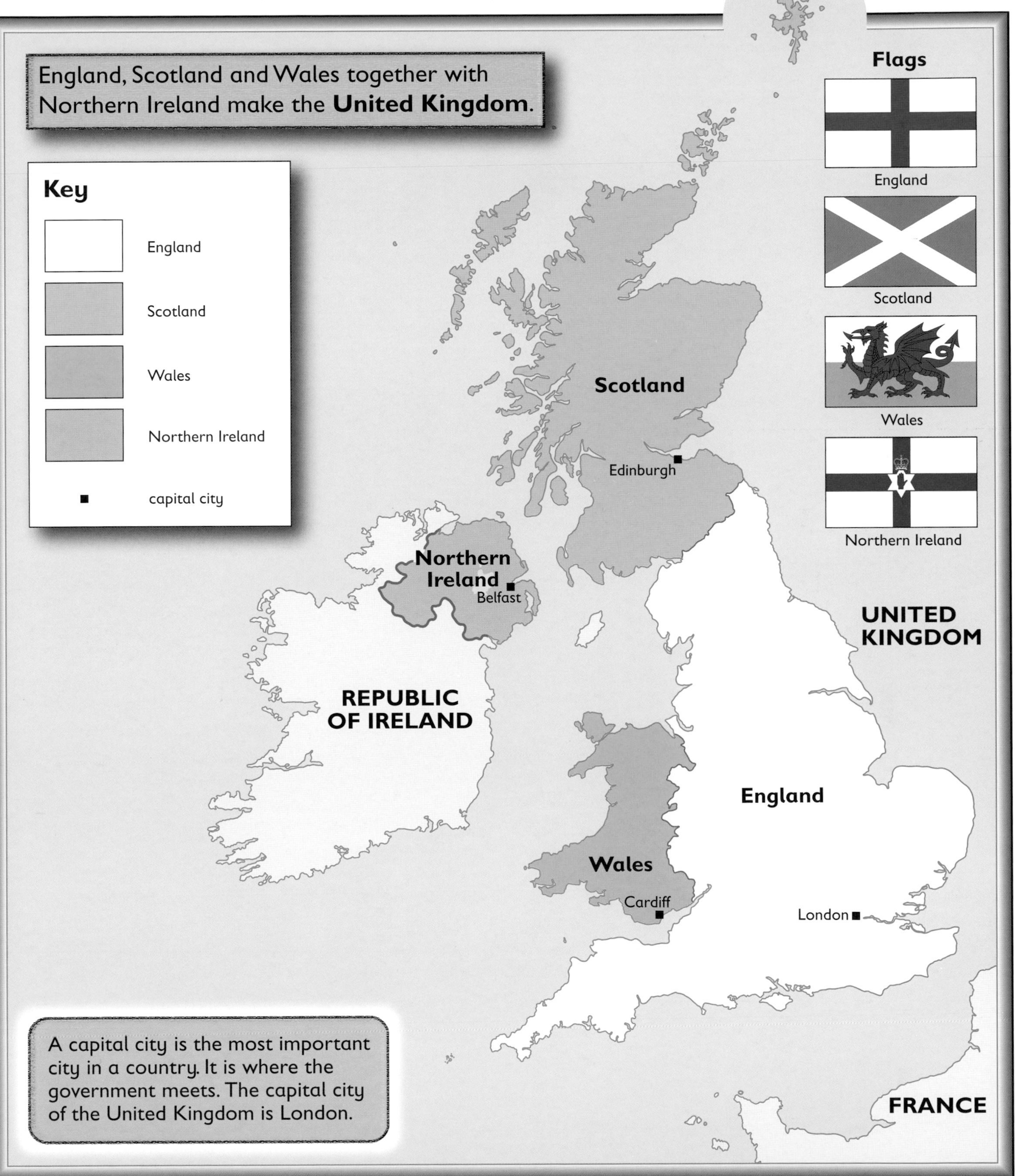

Transverse Mercator Projection

6 Countries of the world

A country is a land with its own people and its own laws.

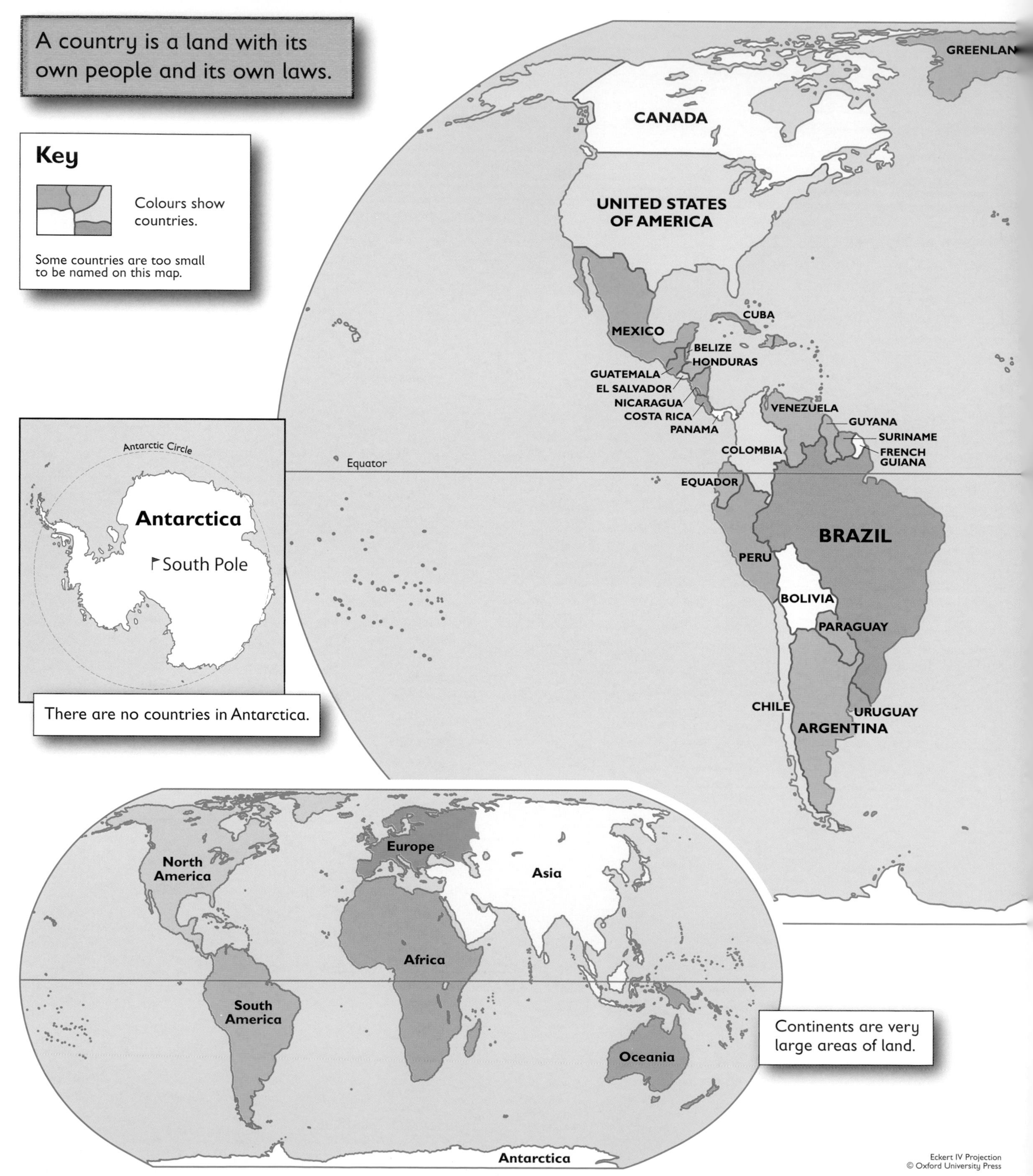

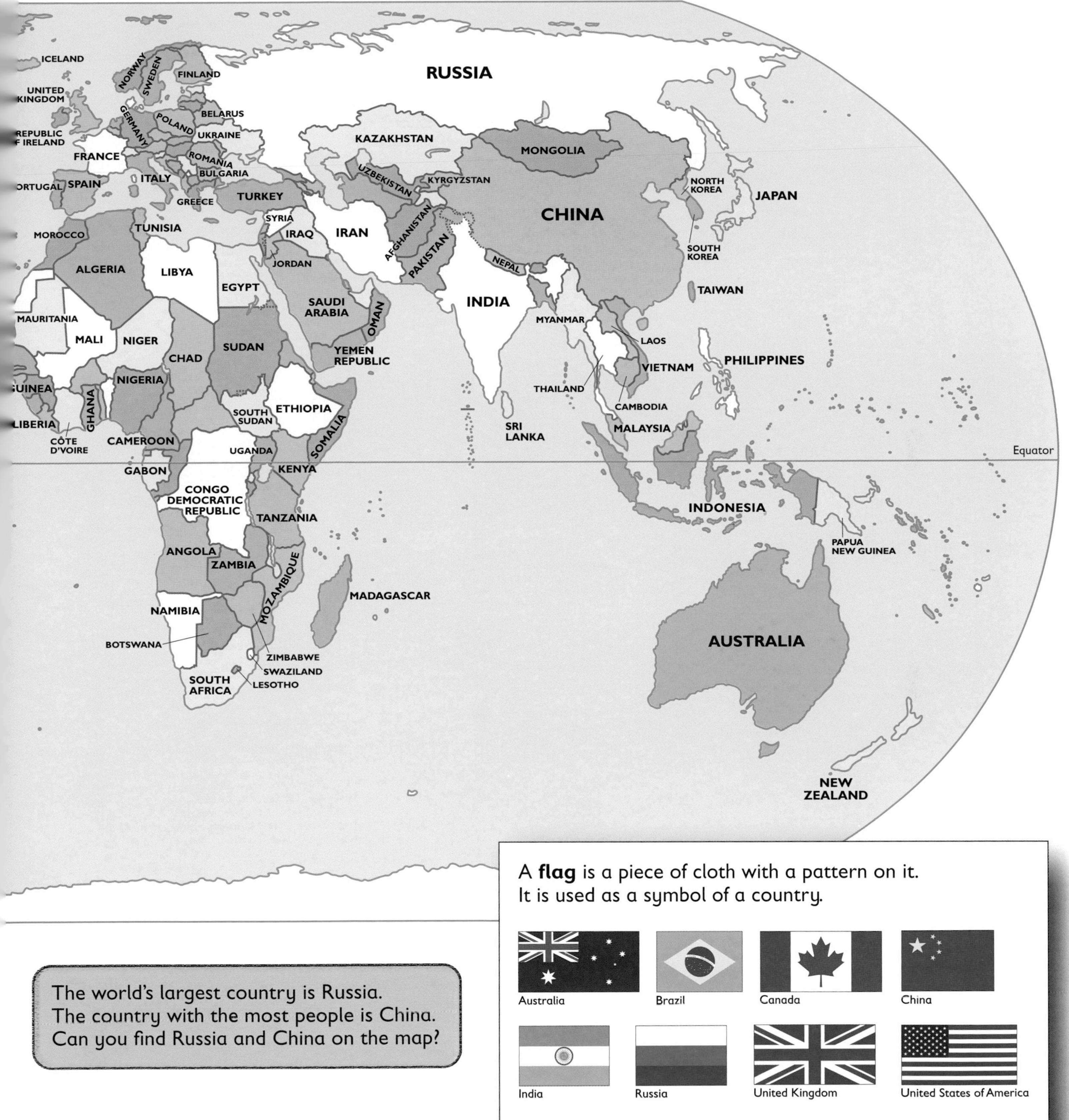

The world's largest country is Russia.
The country with the most people is China.
Can you find Russia and China on the map?

A **flag** is a piece of cloth with a pattern on it.
It is used as a symbol of a country.

Australia

Brazil

Canada

China

India

Russia

United Kingdom

United States of America

Can you find these countries on the map?

8 Mountains, hills and rivers

When you go uphill, the land gets higher. When you go downhill, the land gets lower.

mountains

A mountain is very high land with steep, rocky slopes. Mountains are bigger than hills.

hills

A hill is land that is higher than the land around it. Hills are smaller than mountains.

low land

Land near the sea is low.

rivers

A river is a lot of water that flows down to the sea.

Mountains and rivers in the British Isles

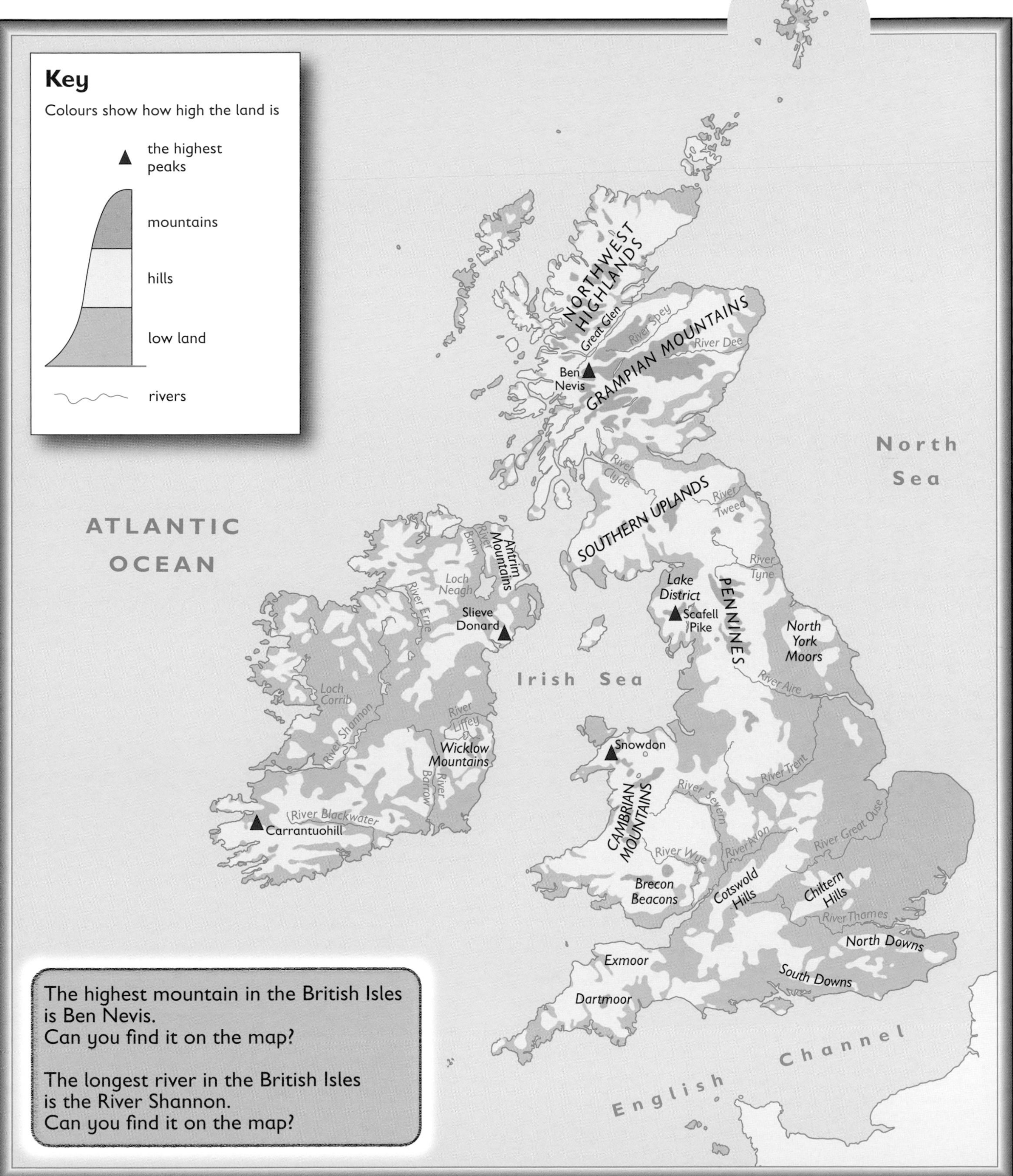

The highest mountain in the British Isles is Ben Nevis.
Can you find it on the map?

The longest river in the British Isles is the River Shannon.
Can you find it on the map?

Transverse Mercator Projection

10 Mountains and rivers around the world

Many mountains and rivers in other parts of the world are much bigger than those in the British Isles.

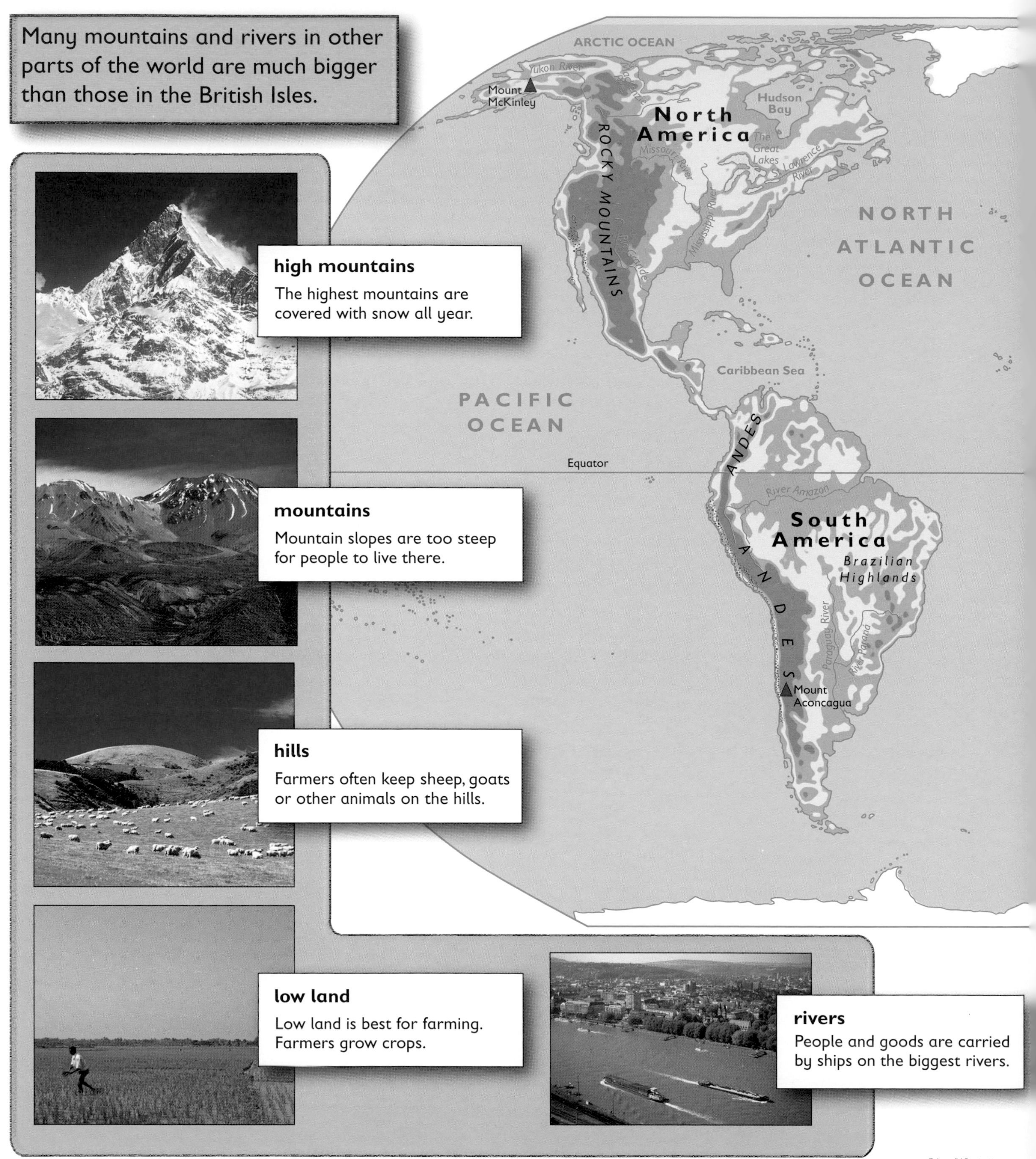

high mountains

The highest mountains are covered with snow all year.

mountains

Mountain slopes are too steep for people to live there.

hills

Farmers often keep sheep, goats or other animals on the hills.

low land

Low land is best for farming. Farmers grow crops.

rivers

People and goods are carried by ships on the biggest rivers.

Eckert IV Projection

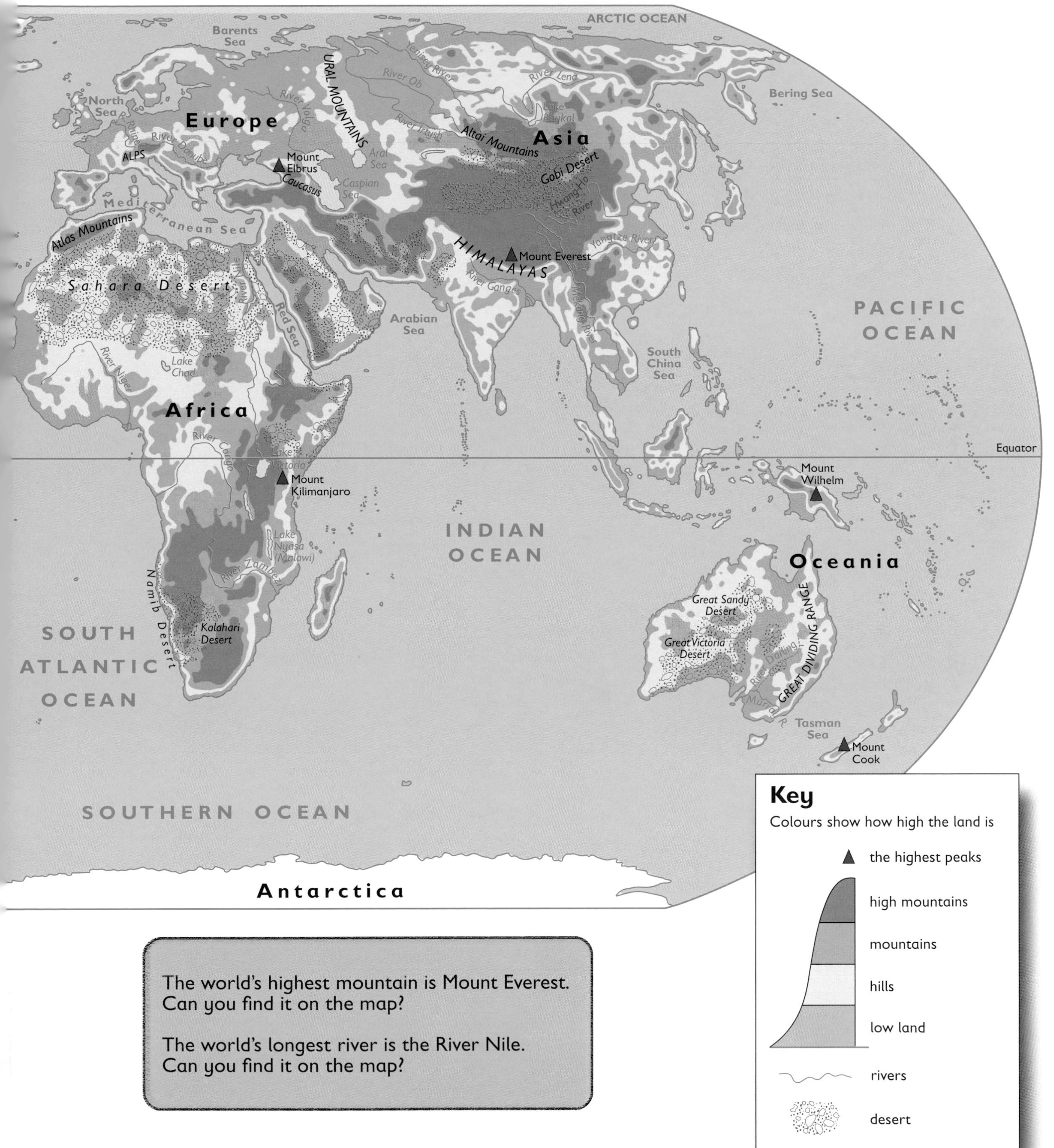

The world's highest mountain is Mount Everest. Can you find it on the map?

The world's longest river is the River Nile. Can you find it on the map?

12 By the sea

Where the land meets the sea is called the **coast**.

beach

A beach is land by the edge of the sea that is covered with sand or small stones.

cliff

A cliff is a hill with one side that goes straight down to the sea.

port

A port is a place on the coast where ships come and go.

seaside resort

A seaside resort is a place where you go for a seaside holiday.

By the sea in the United Kingdom

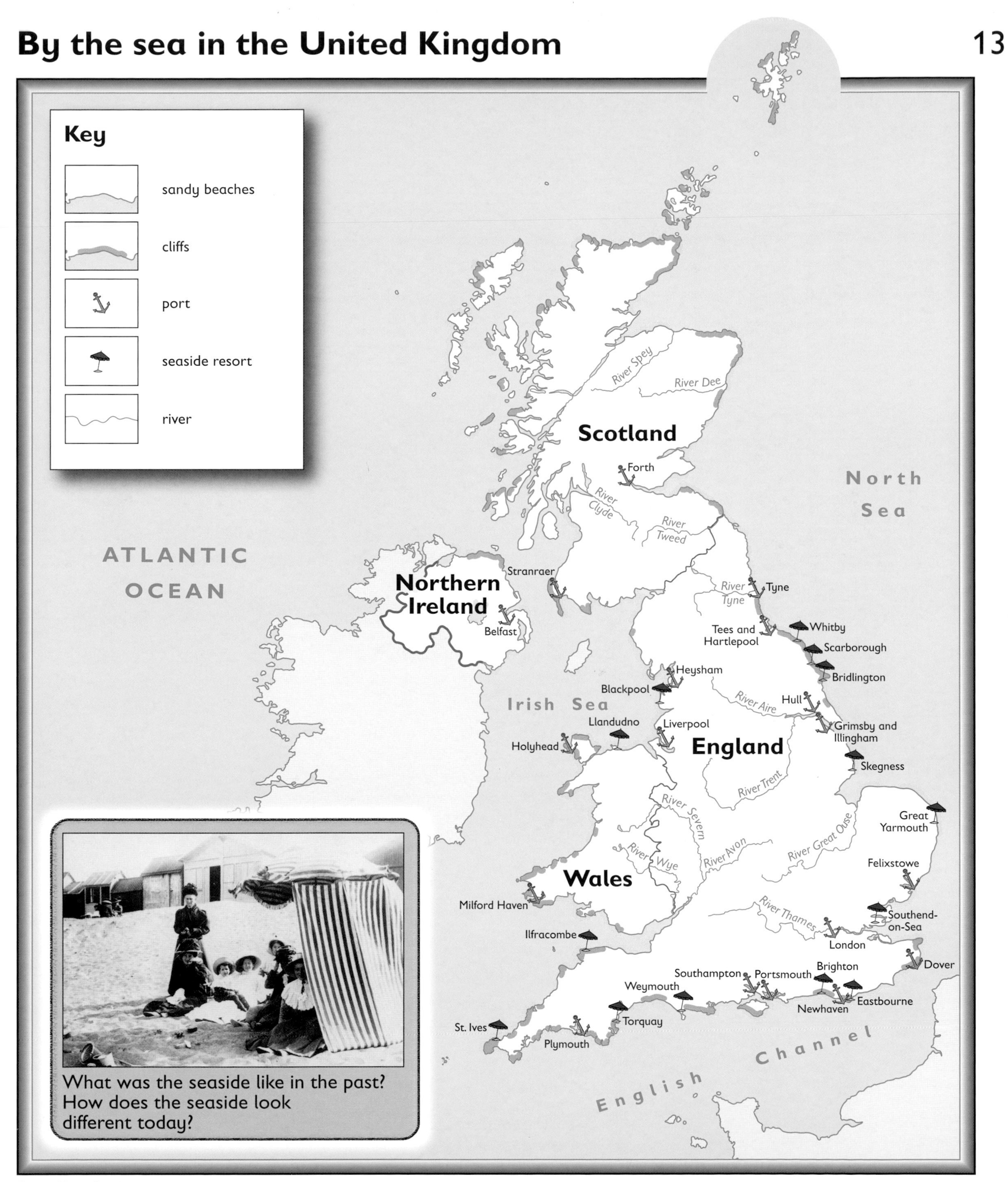

What was the seaside like in the past? How does the seaside look different today?

Transverse Mercator Projection

14 Our weather

The weather is how it is outside, for example, whether it is hot or cold, sunny or raining.

spring			summer			autumn			winter		
March	April	May	June	July	August	September	October	November	December	January	February

The year has twelve months and four seasons.

The weather in the British Isles

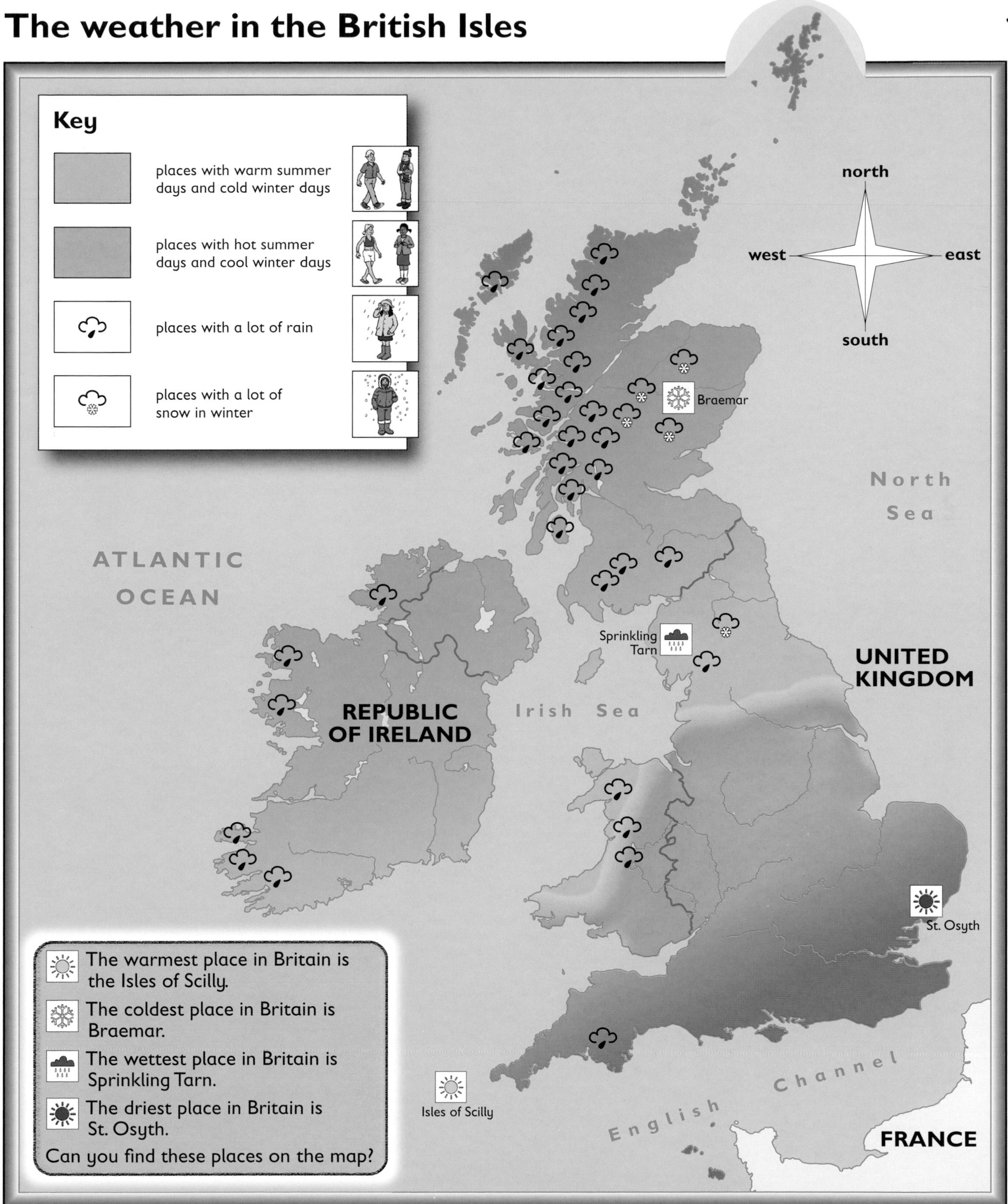

Transverse Mercator Projection

Weather around the world

Homes and clothes around the world are designed according to what the weather is usually like.

Hot places
Long loose clothes keep this man cool.

Cold places
Hats and fur hoods keep these girls warm.

Rainy places
Heavy rain has made the roads flood.

Eckert IV Projection

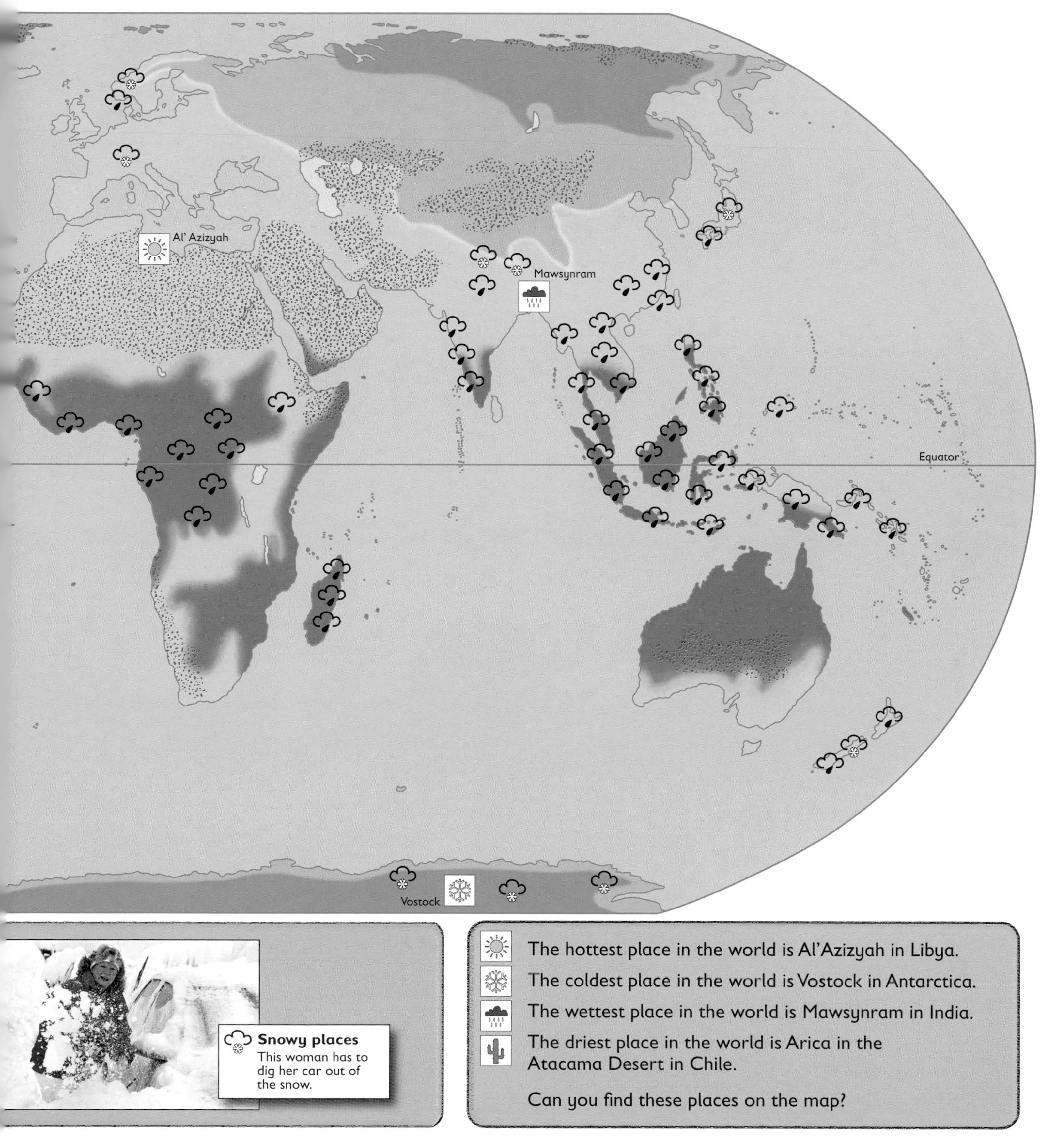

Snowy places
This woman has to dig her car out of the snow.

The hottest place in the world is Al'Azizyah in Libya.

The coldest place in the world is Vostock in Antarctica.

The wettest place in the world is Mawsynram in India.

The driest place in the world is Arica in the Atacama Desert in Chile.

Can you find these places on the map?

18 Our environment

The environment is the air, land and water that surrounds us. We need to protect the environment.

farmland

Farmers use the land to produce food by growing crops and keeping animals.

forest and woodland

Land used to grow trees for wood.

built-up areas

Land with houses, shops, factories and other buildings.

National Parks

Beautiful countryside that is specially protected.

Heritage Coast

Beautiful coastal scenery that is specially protected.

Environments in the United Kingdom

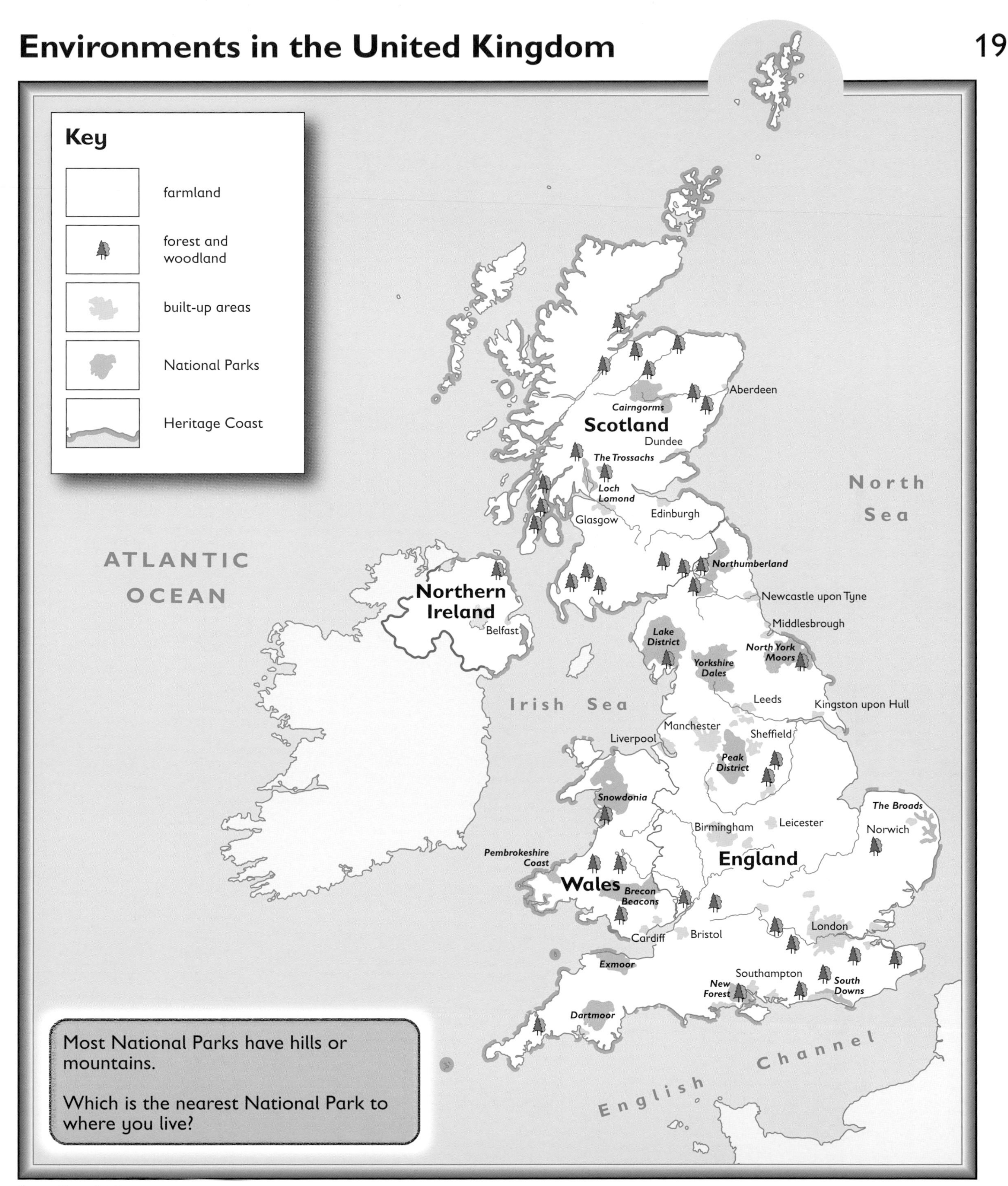

Most National Parks have hills or mountains.

Which is the nearest National Park to where you live?

Transverse Mercator Projection

20 Environments around the world

There are different environments around the world. In some places there are very many plants, in others very few.

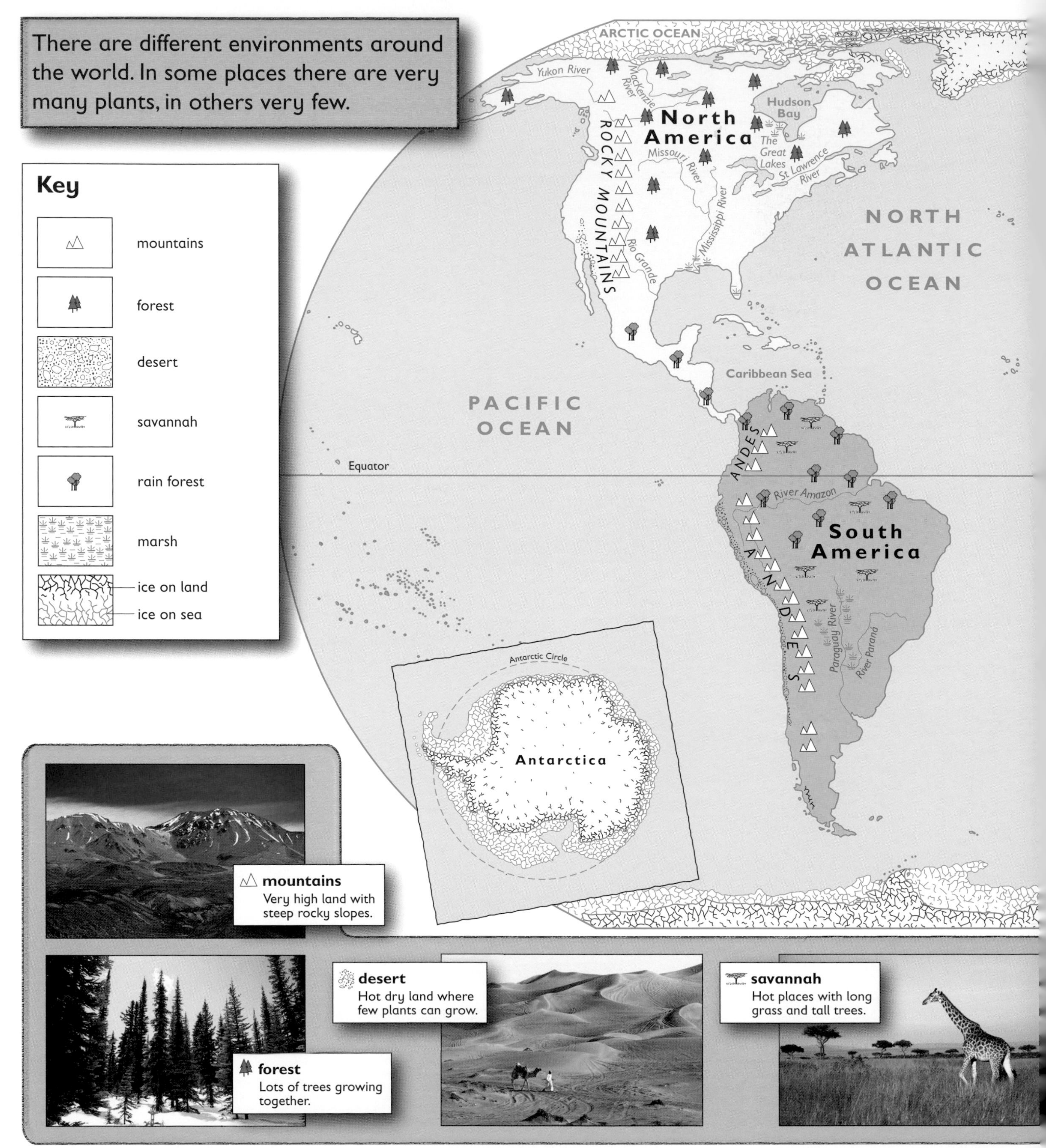

mountains Very high land with steep rocky slopes.

forest Lots of trees growing together.

desert Hot dry land where few plants can grow.

savannah Hot places with long grass and tall trees.

Eckert IV Projection

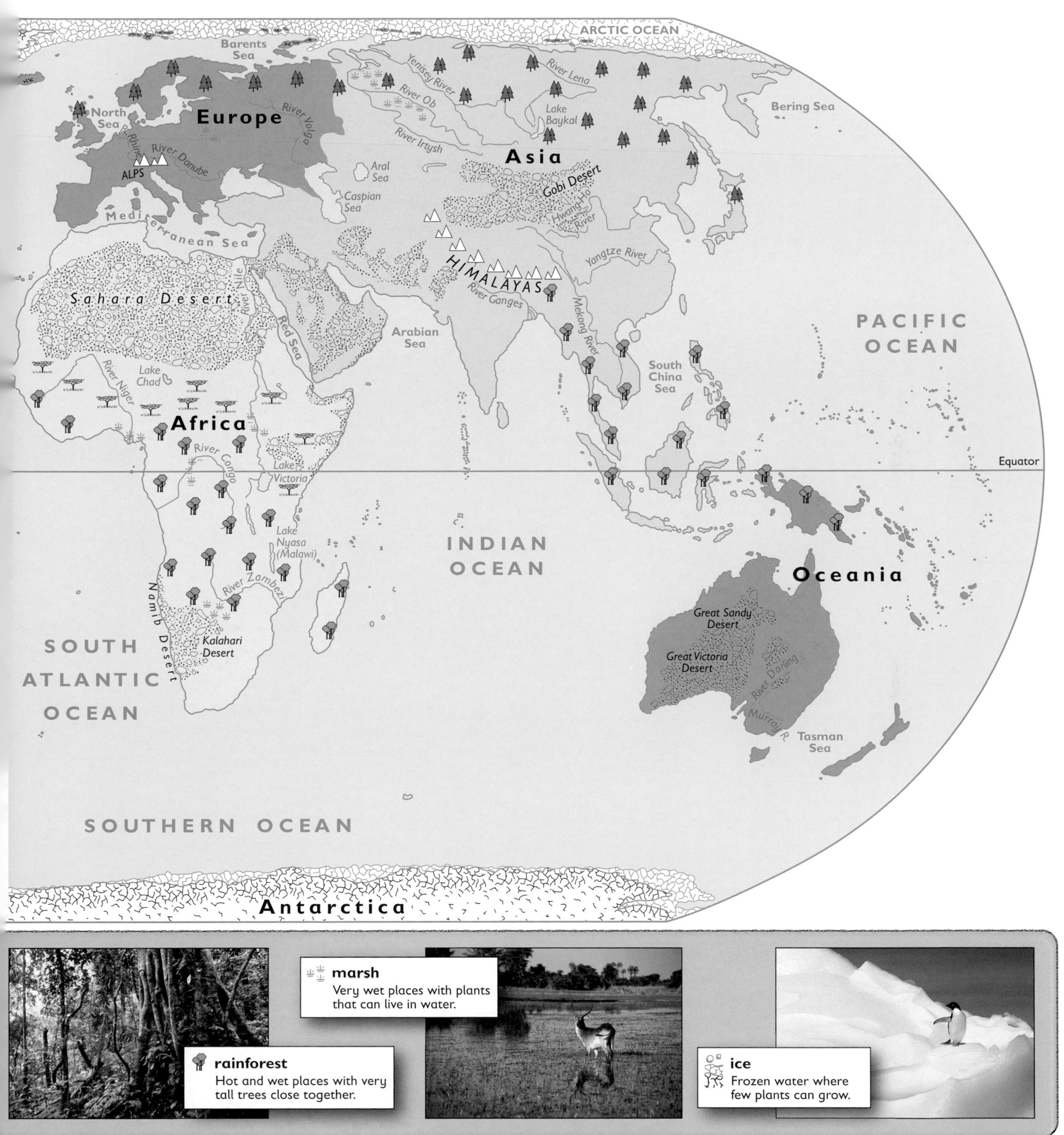

marsh
Very wet places with plants that can live in water.

rainforest
Hot and wet places with very tall trees close together.

ice
Frozen water where few plants can grow.

22 Animals around the world

Eckert IV Projection

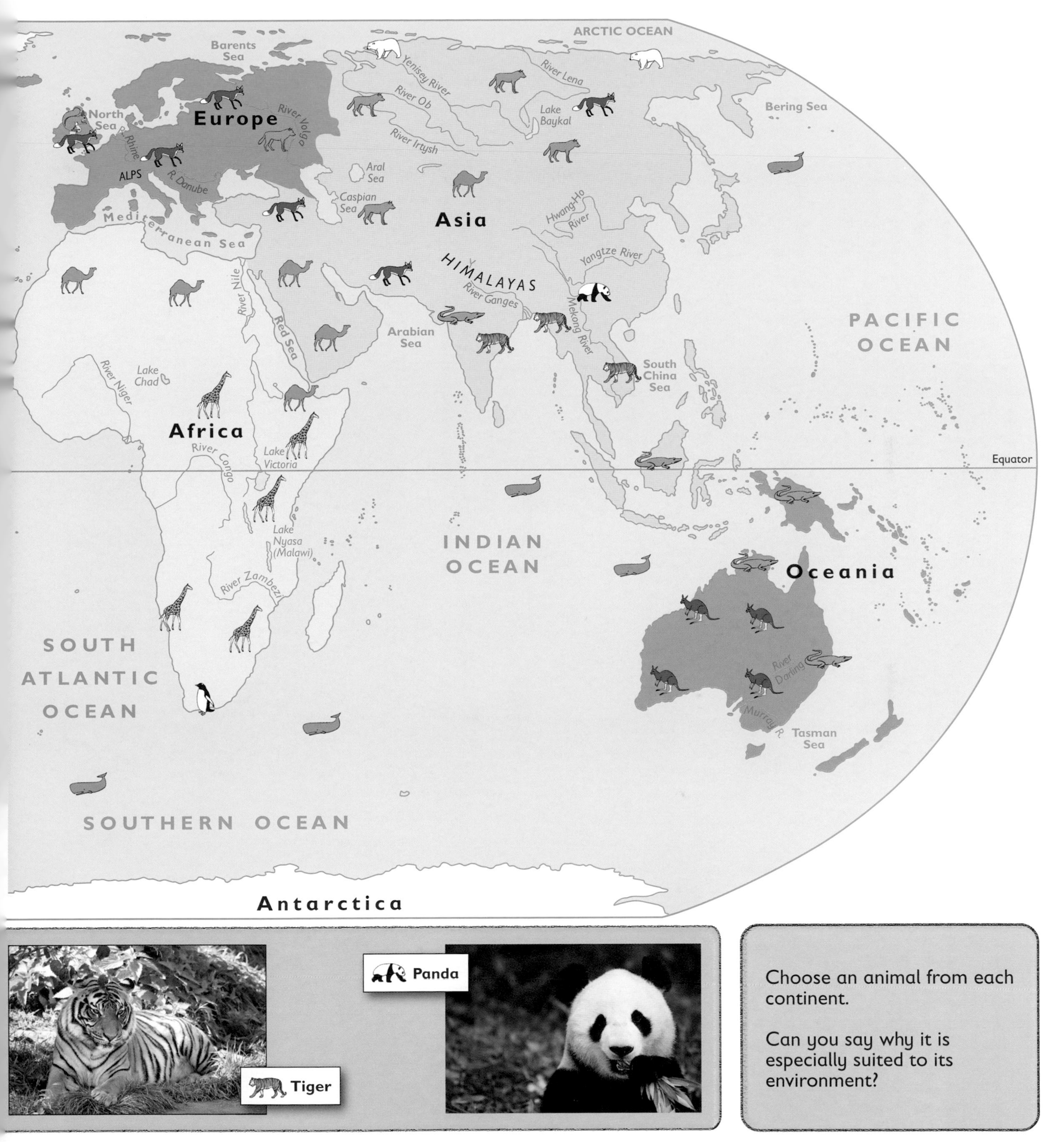

Choose an animal from each continent.

Can you say why it is especially suited to its environment?

24 Towns and cities

A town is a place with a lot of houses, shops, factories, offices and other buildings. A city is a very large town. Towns and cities are built-up areas.

built-up area

This photograph shows part of Birmingham seen from the air. Can you find:

- A street with houses
- A football stadium
- A main road
- A park
- A carpark
- A railway line

Towns and cities in the United Kingdom

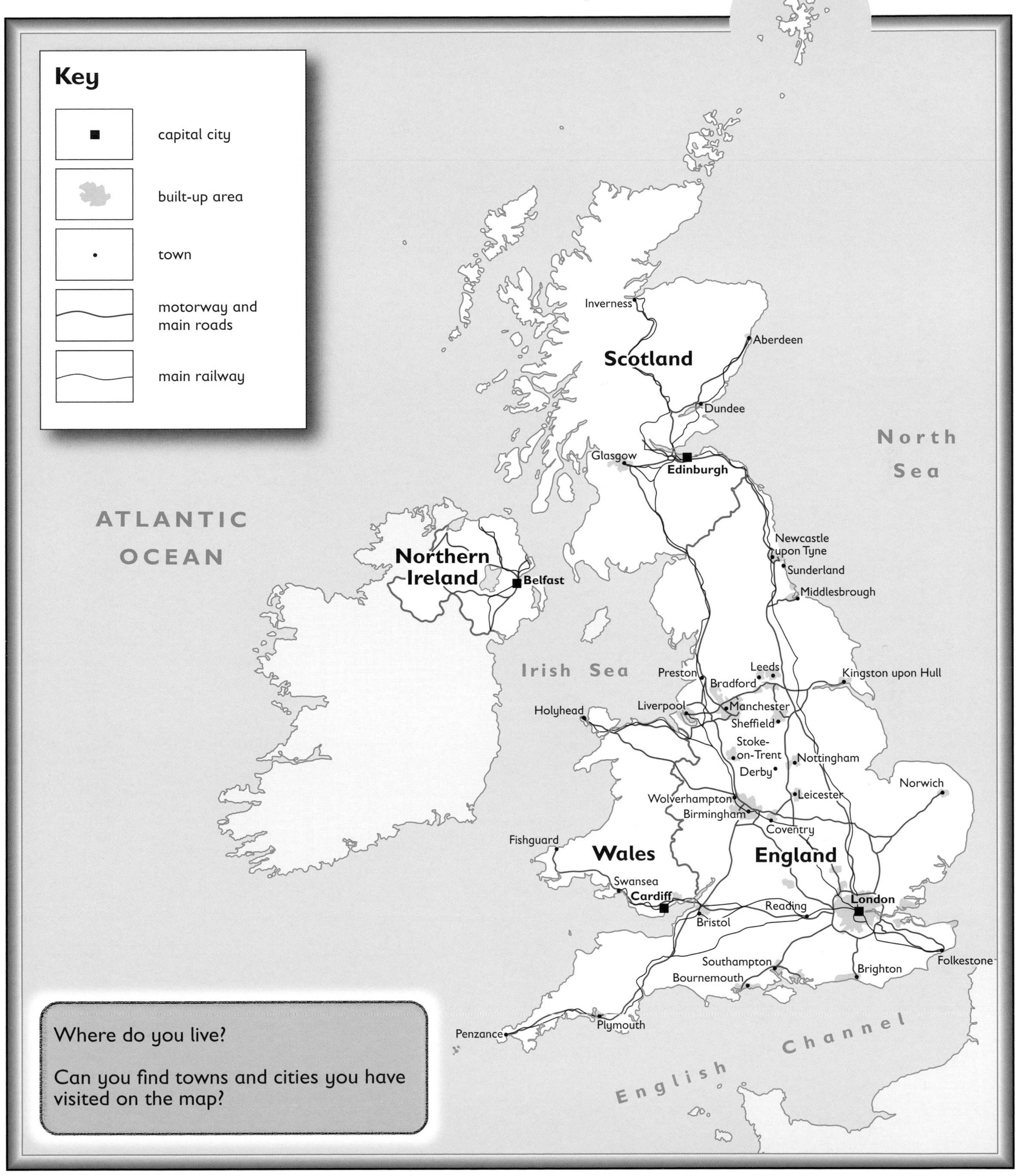

Transverse Mercator Projection

Where people live in the world

Some places in the world are very crowded. Other places have very few people.

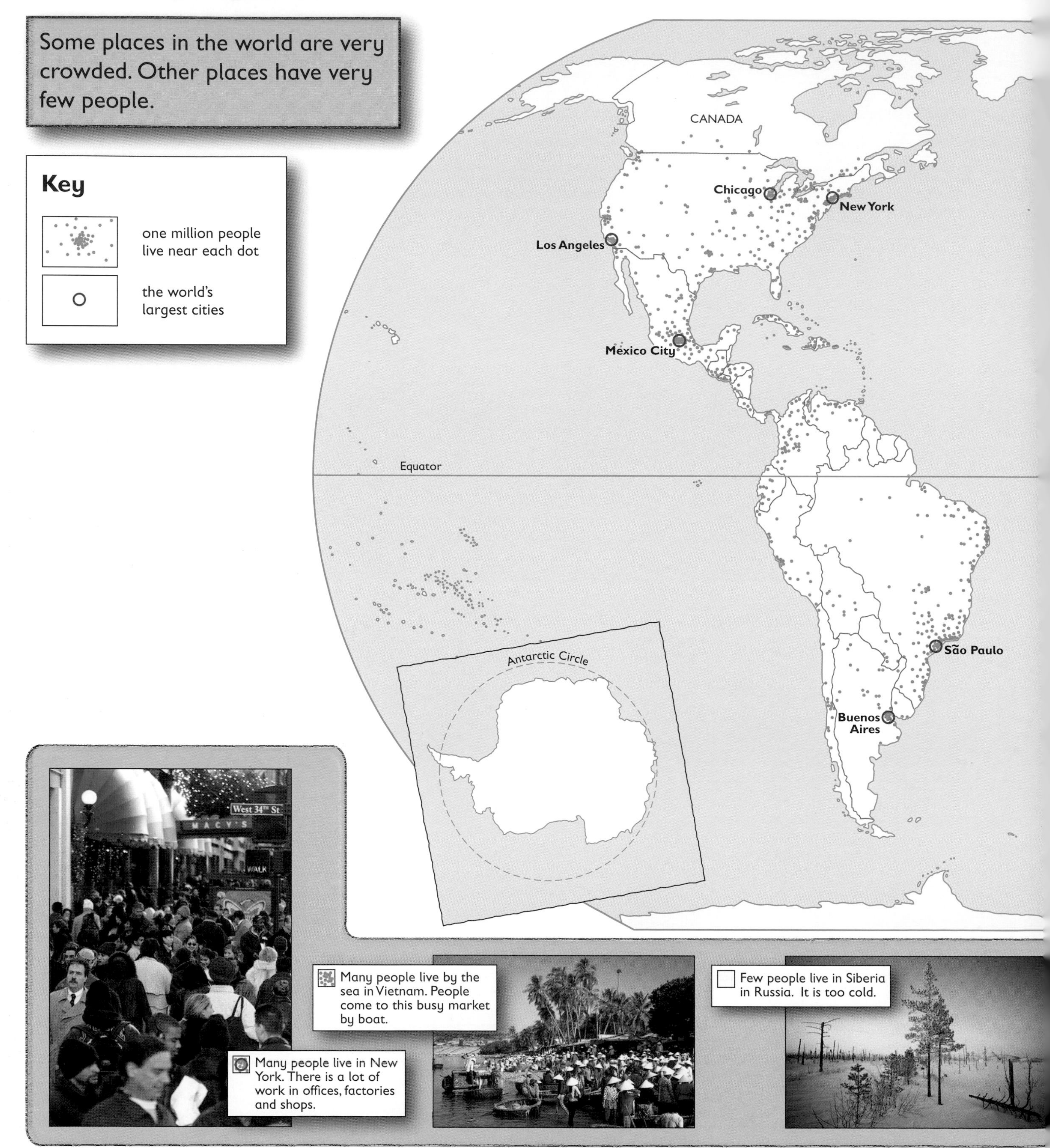

Many people live by the sea in Vietnam. People come to this busy market by boat.

Few people live in Siberia in Russia. It is too cold.

Many people live in New York. There is a lot of work in offices, factories and shops.

Eckert IV Projection

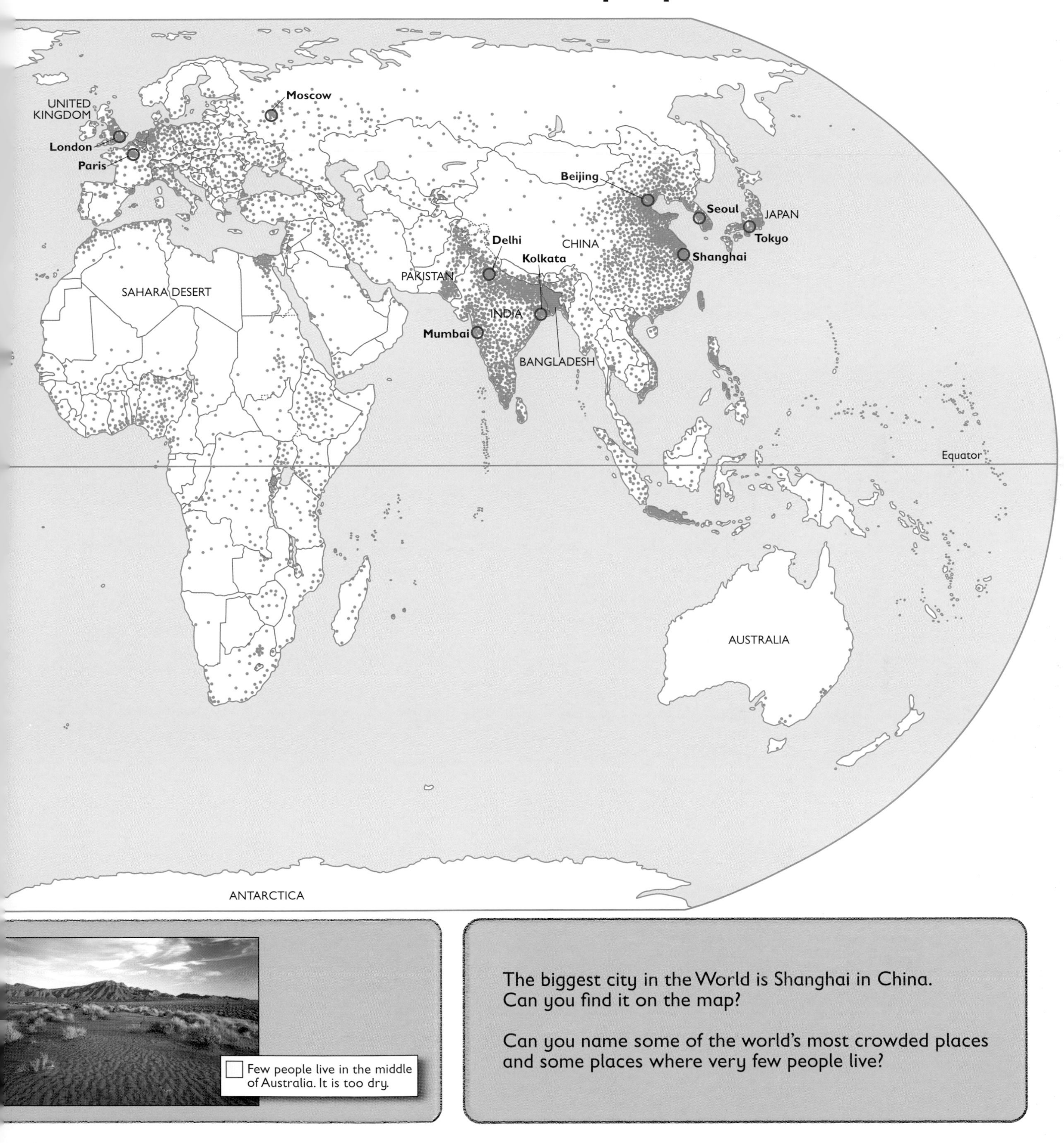

Few people live in the middle of Australia. It is too dry.

The biggest city in the World is Shanghai in China. Can you find it on the map?

Can you name some of the world's most crowded places and some places where very few people live?

28 Holidays

Holidays are time off from school or work. What is there to see and do near where you live?

Castles are large strong buildings with thick stone walls and tall towers. They were built long ago to keep people safe from their enemies.

Cathedrals are big churches that were built by Christians to worship God.

Museums are places where interesting things are kept for people to go and see.

Theme parks are very large outdoor play areas with exciting rides.

Zoos are places where wild animals are kept so that people can go and see them up close.

Some parts of the **countryside and coast** are especially beautiful and many people go on holiday to enjoy the views.

Holidays in the United Kingdom

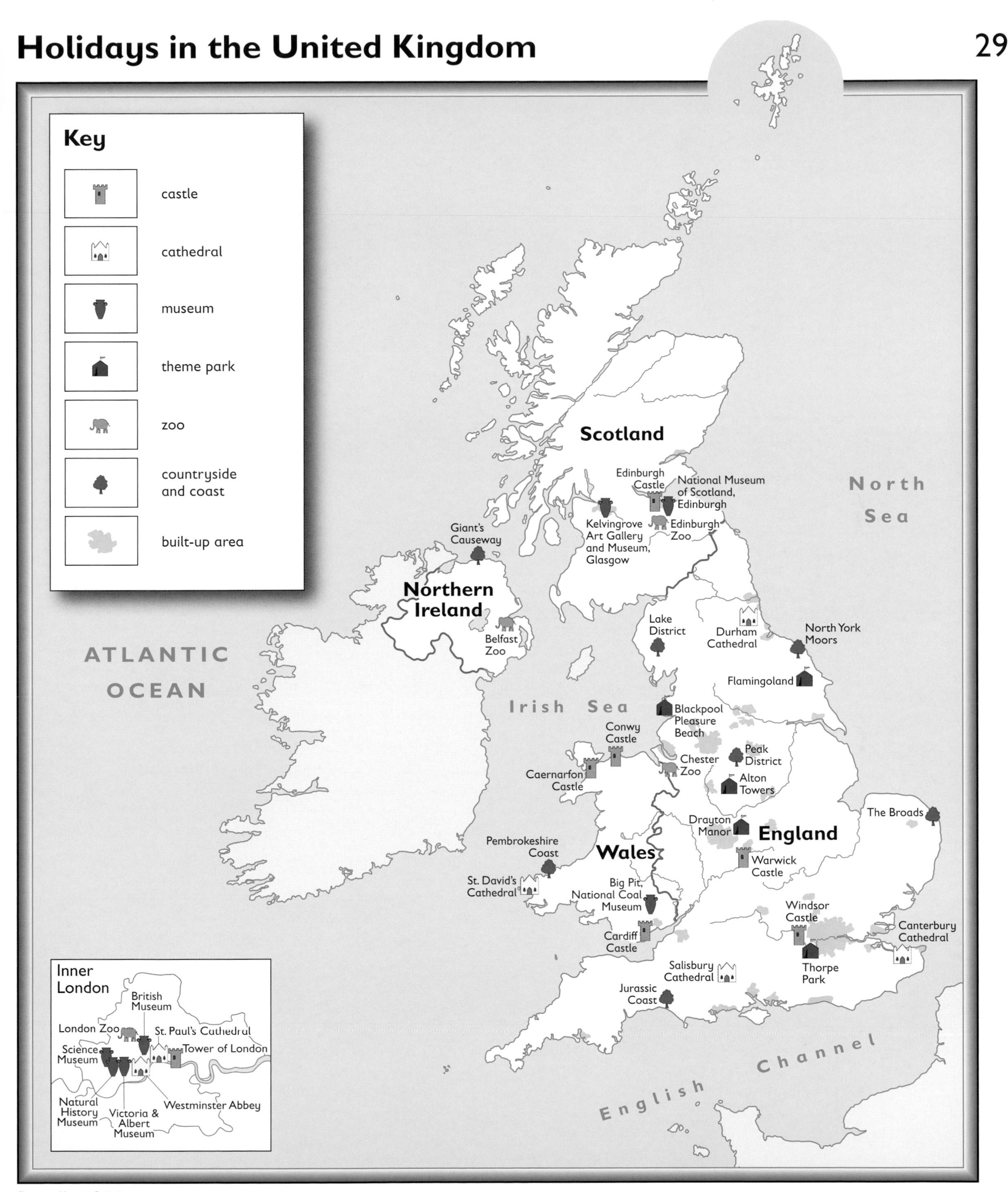

Transverse Mercator Projection

30 Passport to the world

A passport is a booklet that shows who you are and what country you come from. You need a passport to travel to other countries. Here are some places in the world you might like to visit.

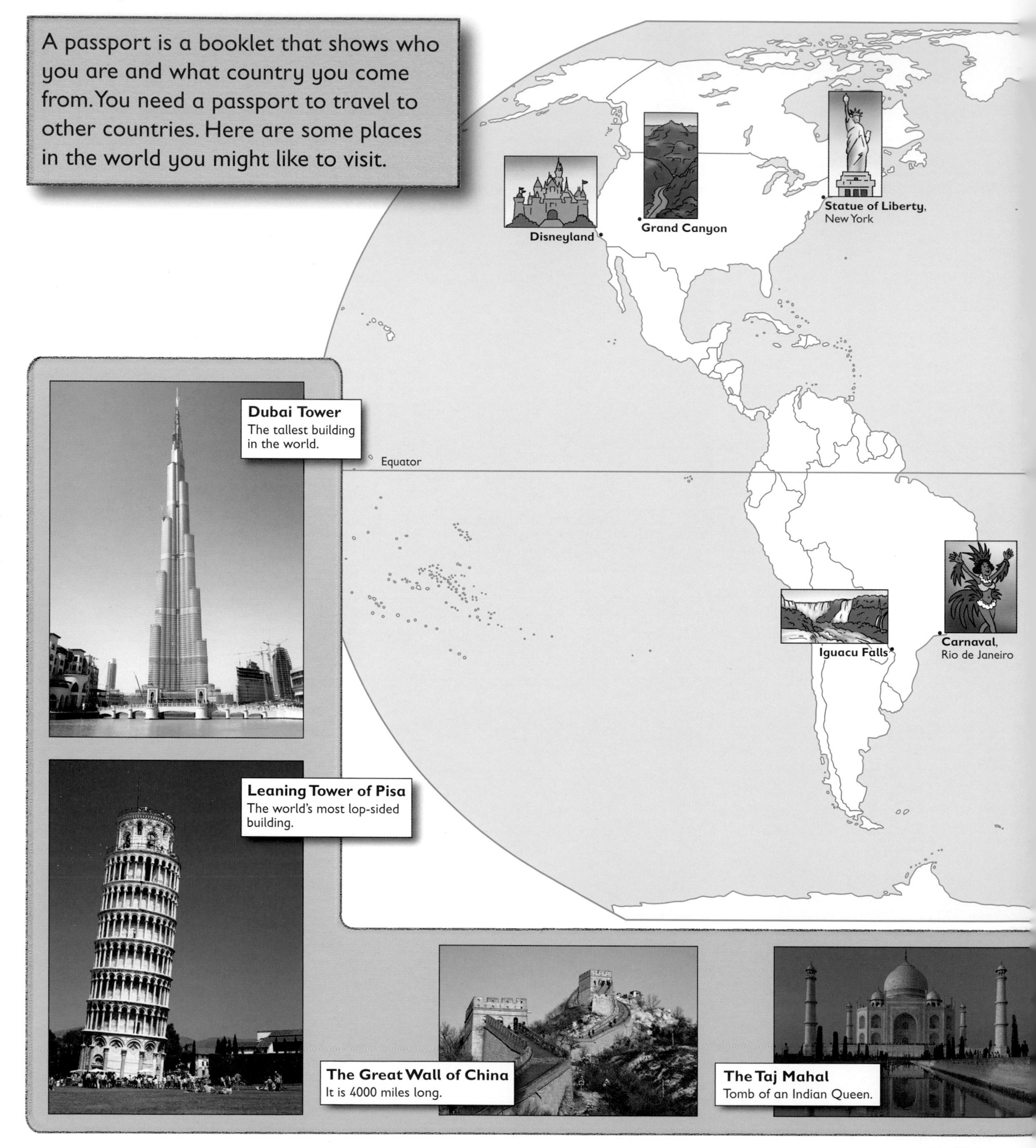

Eckert IV Projection

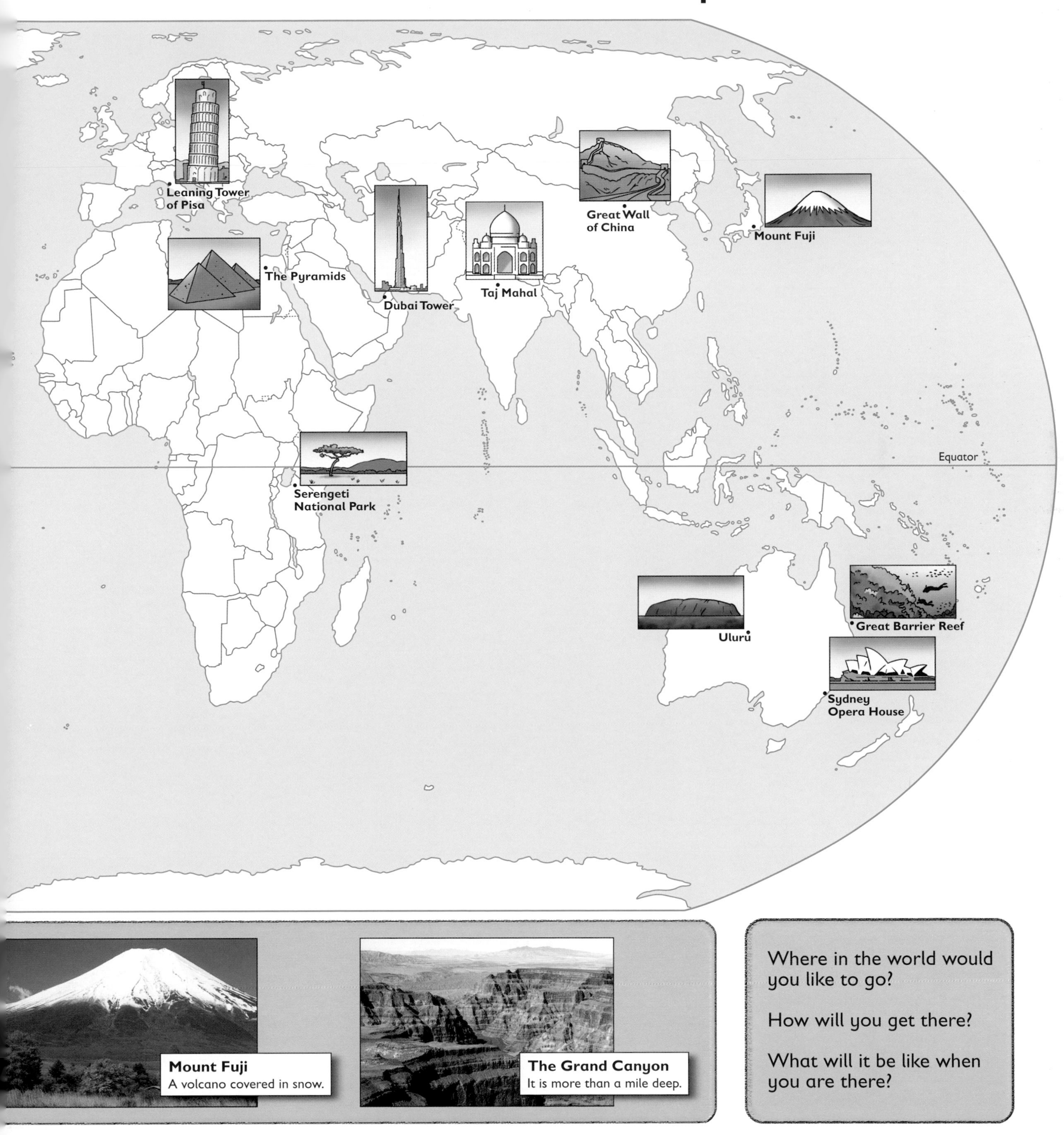

Mount Fuji
A volcano covered in snow.

The Grand Canyon
It is more than a mile deep.

Where in the world would you like to go?

How will you get there?

What will it be like when you are there?

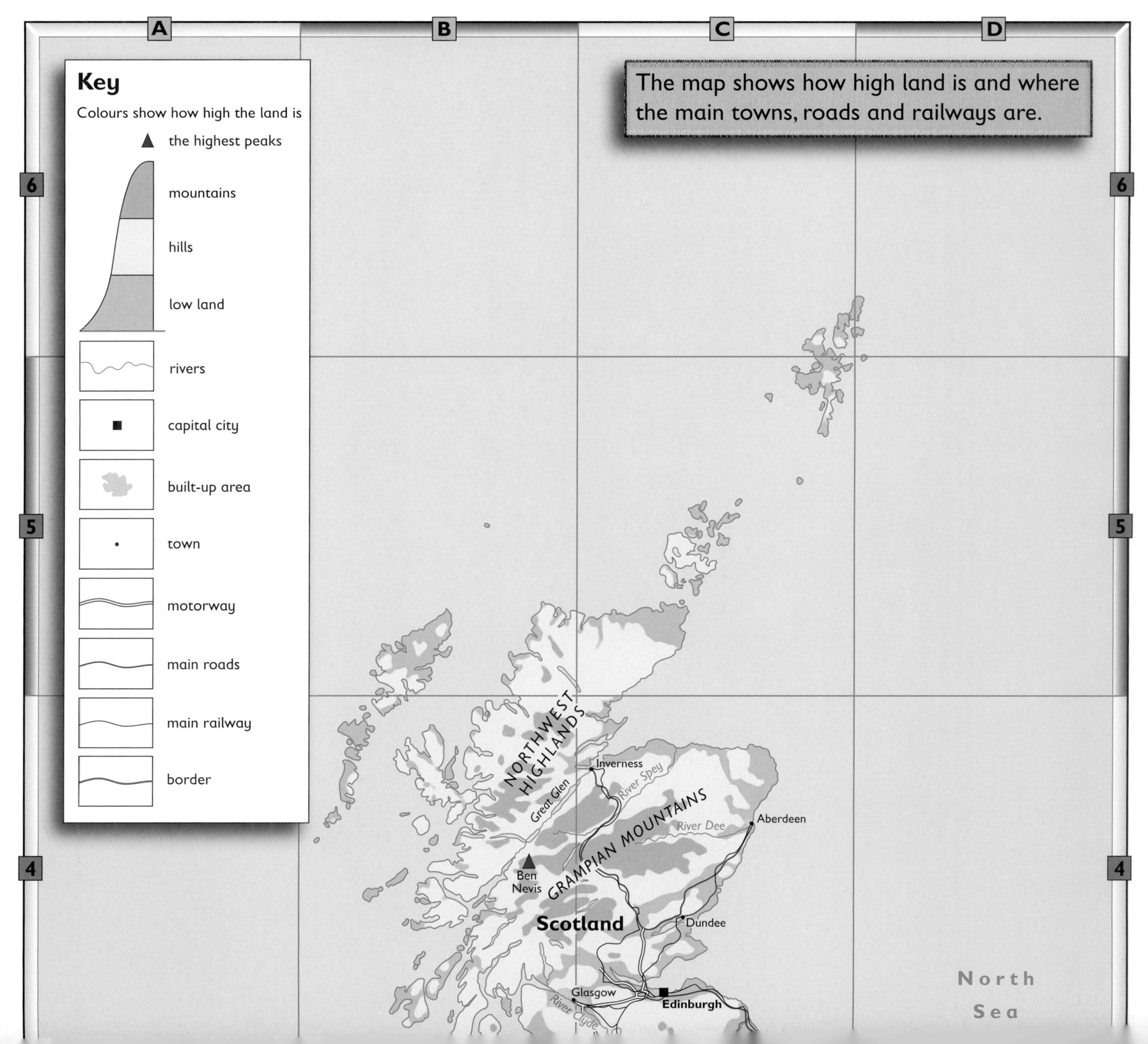

Transverse Mercator Projection

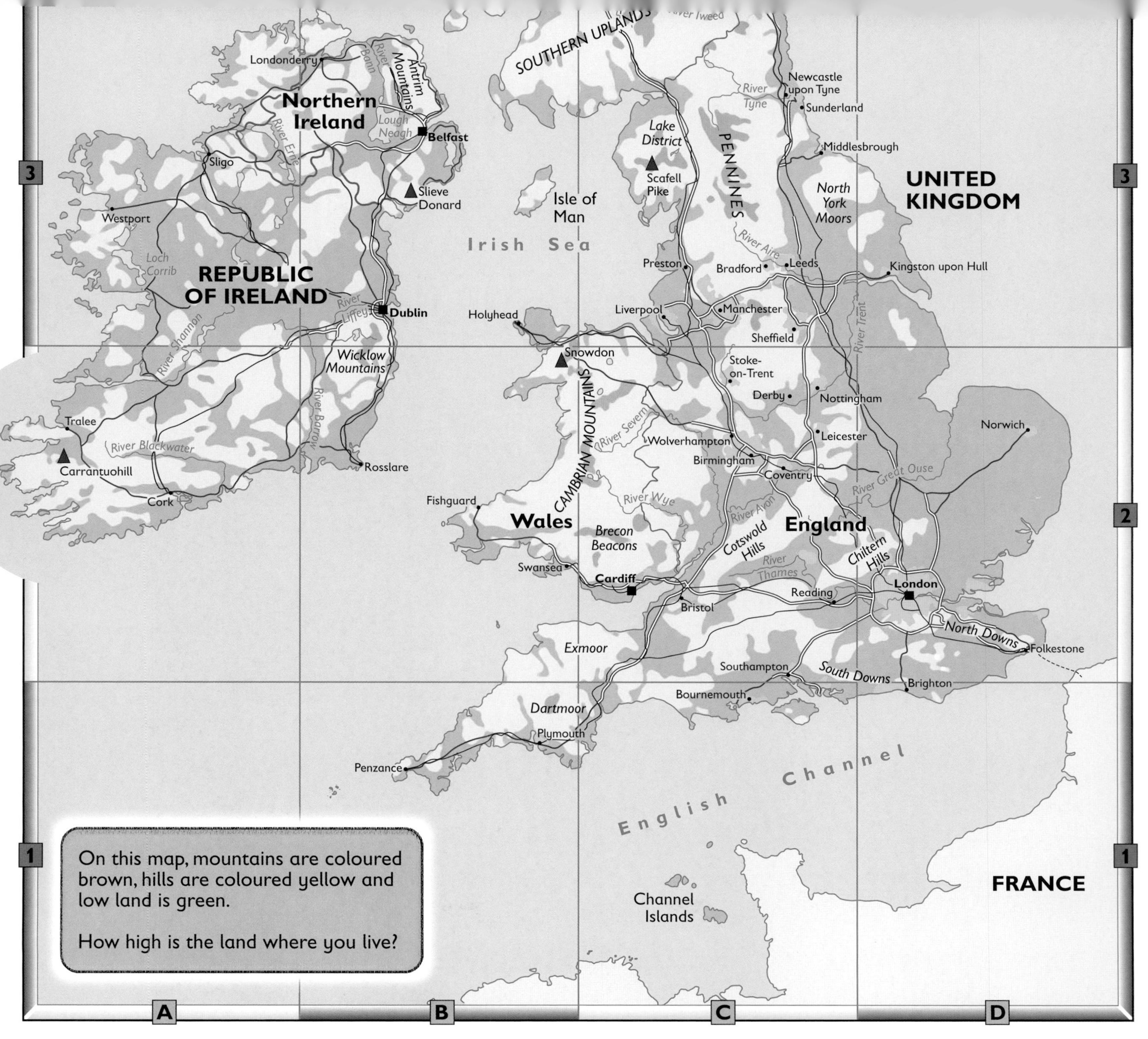

On this map, mountains are coloured brown, hills are coloured yellow and low land is green.
How high is the land where you live?
UNITED KINGDOM
REPUBLIC OF IRELAND
Northern Ireland
England
Wales
FRANCE
Irish Sea
English Channel
Channel Islands
Isle of Man
London
Cardiff
Dublin
Belfast
Newcastle upon Tyne
Sunderland
Middlesbrough
Kingston upon Hull
Leeds
Bradford
Preston
Liverpool
Manchester
Sheffield
Stoke-on-Trent
Derby
Nottingham
Leicester
Coventry
Birmingham
Wolverhampton
Norwich
Reading
Bristol
Swansea
Fishguard
Holyhead
Southampton
Bournemouth
Brighton
Folkestone
Plymouth
Penzance
Londonderry
Sligo
Westport
Tralee
Cork
Rosslare
SOUTHERN UPLANDS
PENNINES
Lake District
Scafell Pike
North York Moors
Snowdon
CAMBRIAN MOUNTAINS
Brecon Beacons
Cotswold Hills
Chiltern Hills
North Downs
South Downs
Exmoor
Dartmoor
Antrim Mountains
Slieve Donard
Wicklow Mountains
Carrantuohill
River Tweed
River Tyne
River Aire
River Trent
River Great Ouse
River Severn
River Wye
River Avon
River Thames
River Bann
Lough Neagh
River Erne
River Liffey
River Barrow
River Shannon
Loch Corrib
River Blackwater
A
B
C
D
1
2
3

Modified Gall Projection

There are many European languages.

Many people go on holiday to Spain because the weather in summer is hot and dry.

Painted Easter eggs are popular in many European countries.

Do you know what language people speak in each of these countries?

France
Spain
Greece
Italy
The Netherlands

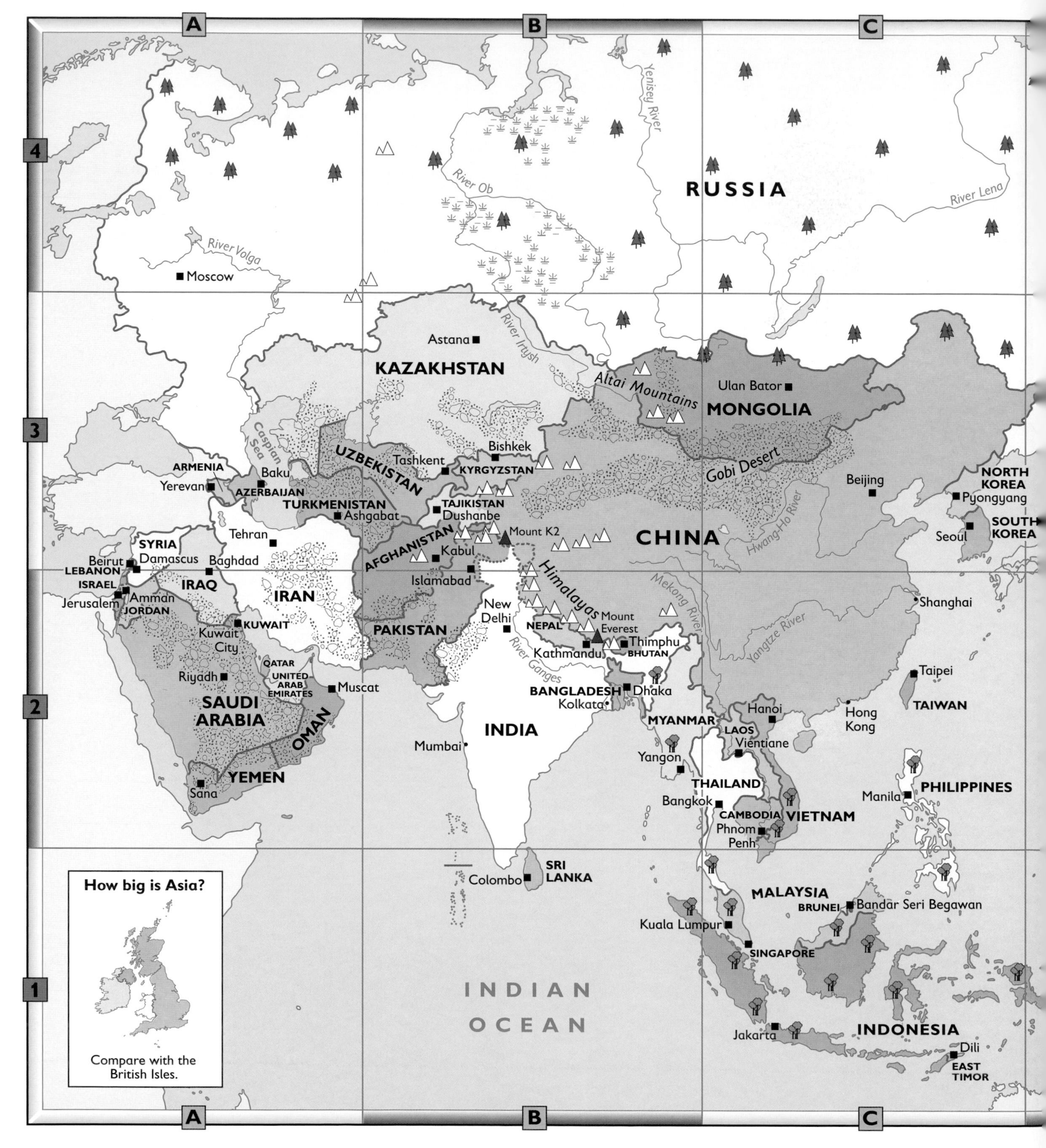

Modified Gall Projection

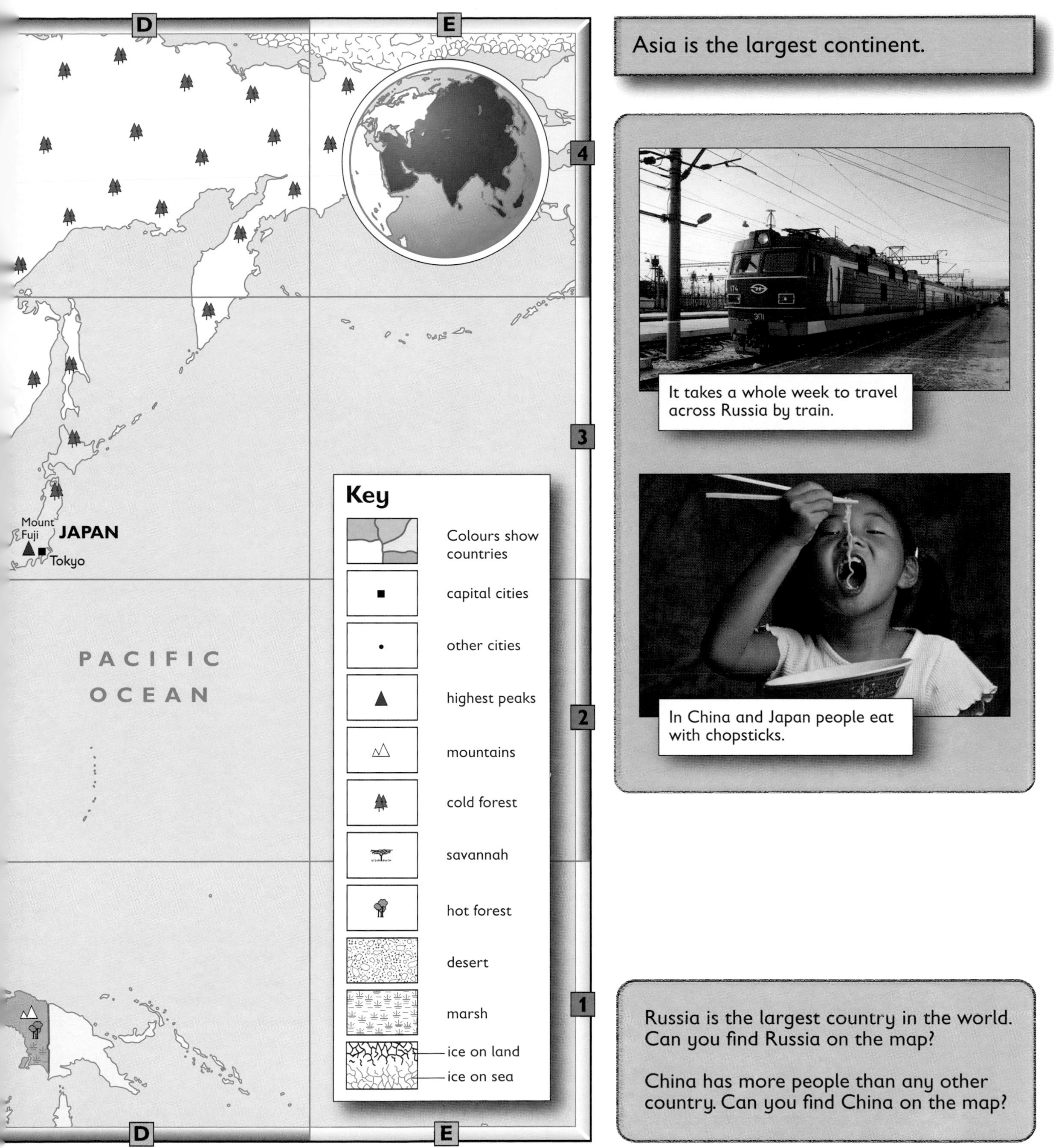

Asia is the largest continent.

It takes a whole week to travel across Russia by train.

In China and Japan people eat with chopsticks.

Russia is the largest country in the world. Can you find Russia on the map?

China has more people than any other country. Can you find China on the map?

North America

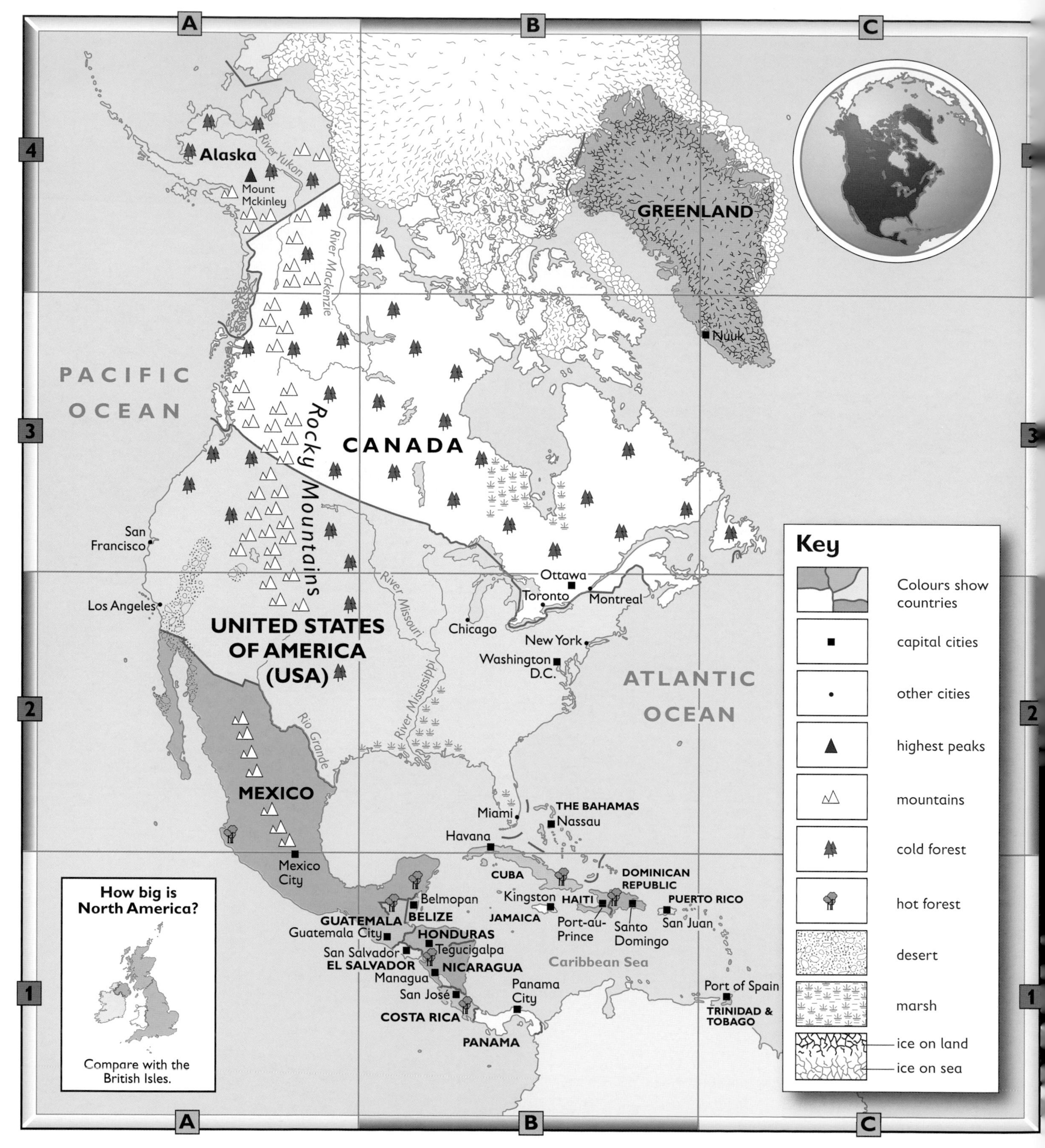

Oblique Mercator Projection

The United States of America is the richest country in the world.

The Statue of Liberty stands in New York harbour.

Mexico is famous for its spicy food.

The president of the United States lives in the White House.

School buses in the United States and Canada are painted yellow.

The capital of the United States is Washington D.C. Can you find it on the map?

South America

Oblique Mercator Projection

In the Amazon rainforest it is very hot and it rains every day. Trees in the forest are being cut down.

Carnaval in Brazil is a street party that lasts for five days.

These giant tortoises live in the Galapagos Islands.

The Amazon rainforest has very many plants, animals and insects.

Angel Falls in Venezuela is the world's highest waterfall.

The Atacama Desert is the driest place in the world. Can you find it on the map?

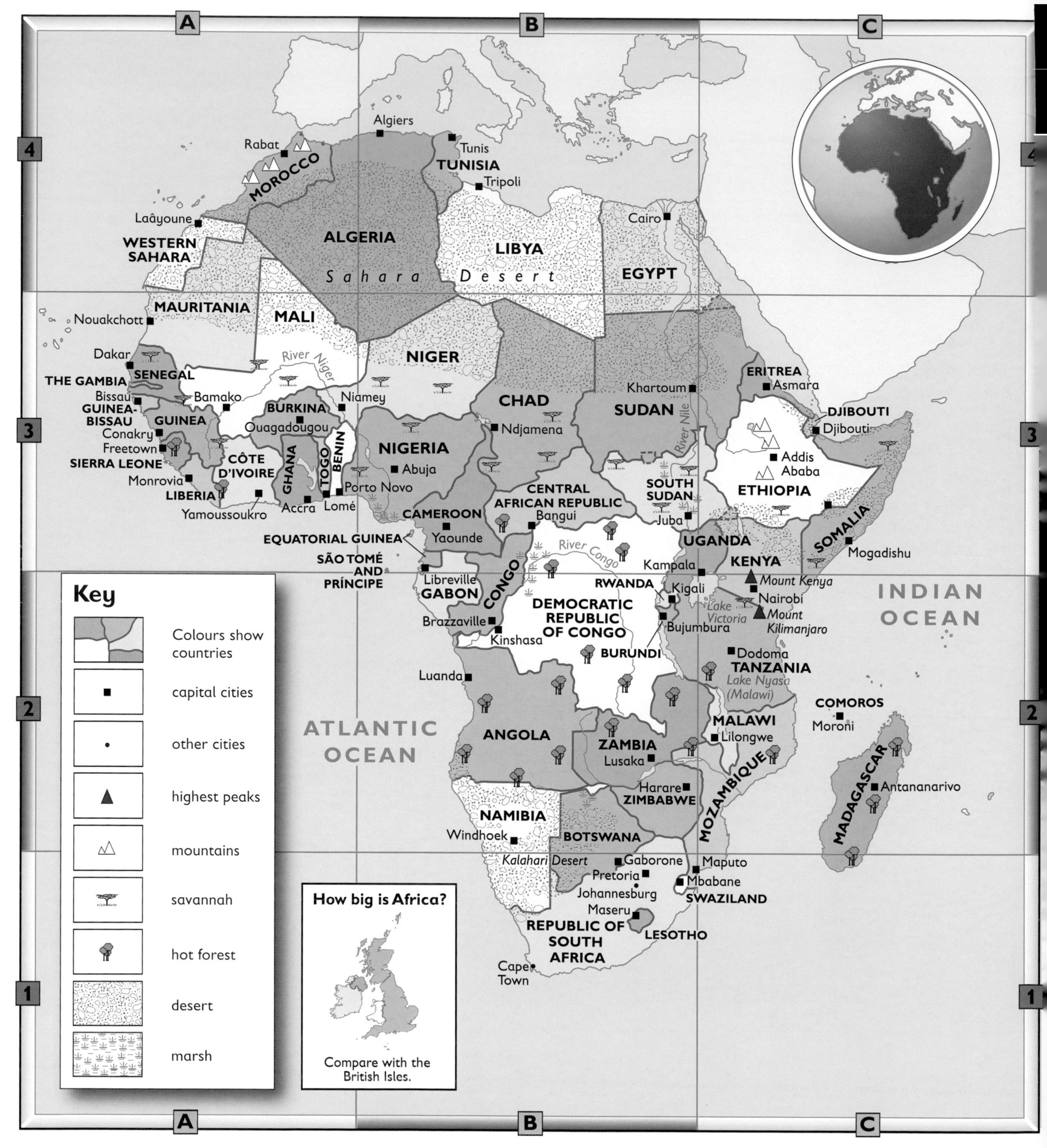

Zenithal Equal Area Projection

Africa is a continent with many different countries and many different environments.

The savannah is dry. These wildebeest and zebra are thirsty.

The pyramids are where ancient Egyptians buried their dead kings.

These girls are getting water from the well.

Going shopping on market day in Mali.

The Sahara Desert is the largest desert in the world. Can you find it on the map?

Oceania

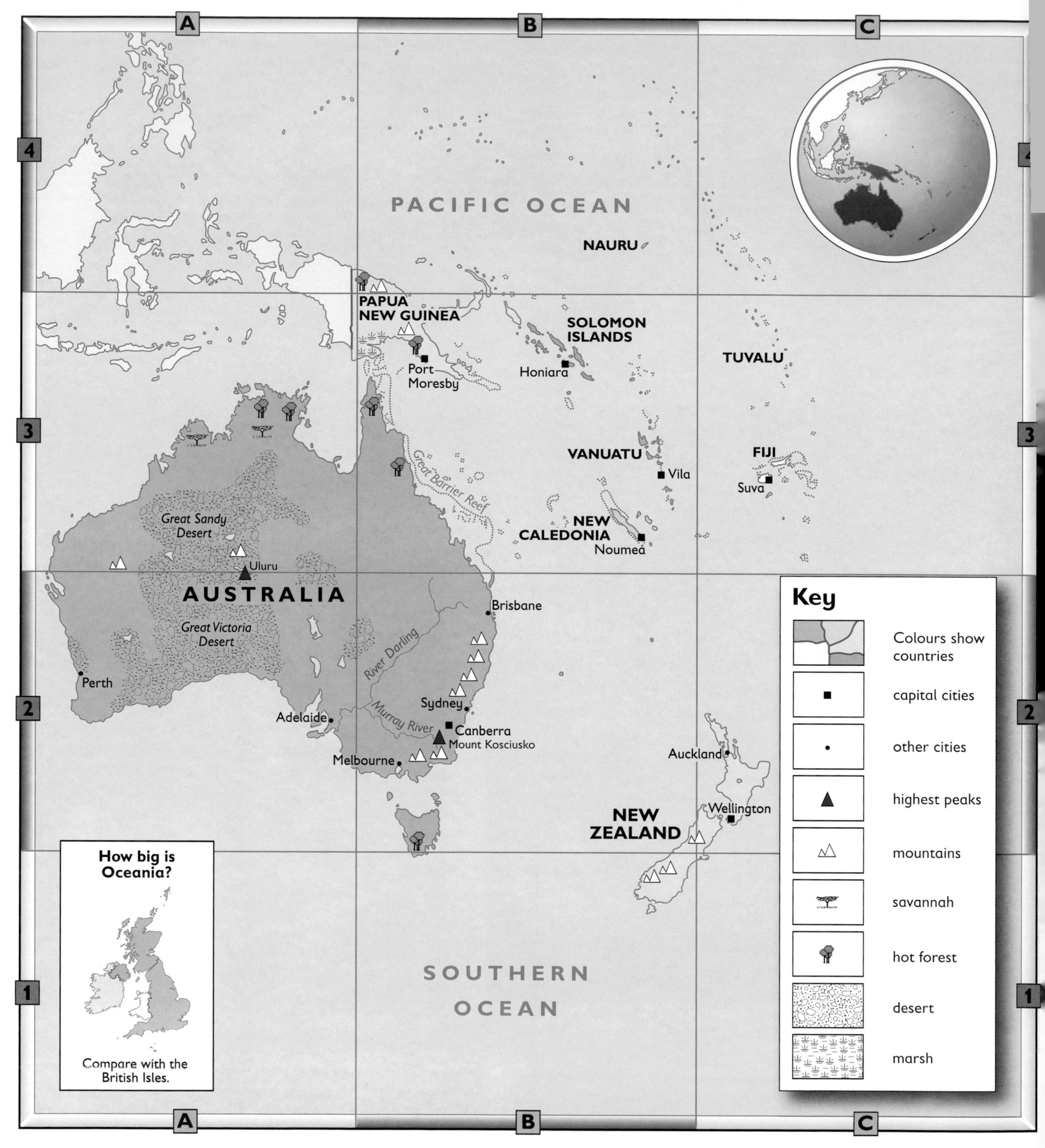

Modified Gall Projection

Australia is on the other side of the Earth to the British Isles. When it is winter in Britain, it is summer in Australia.

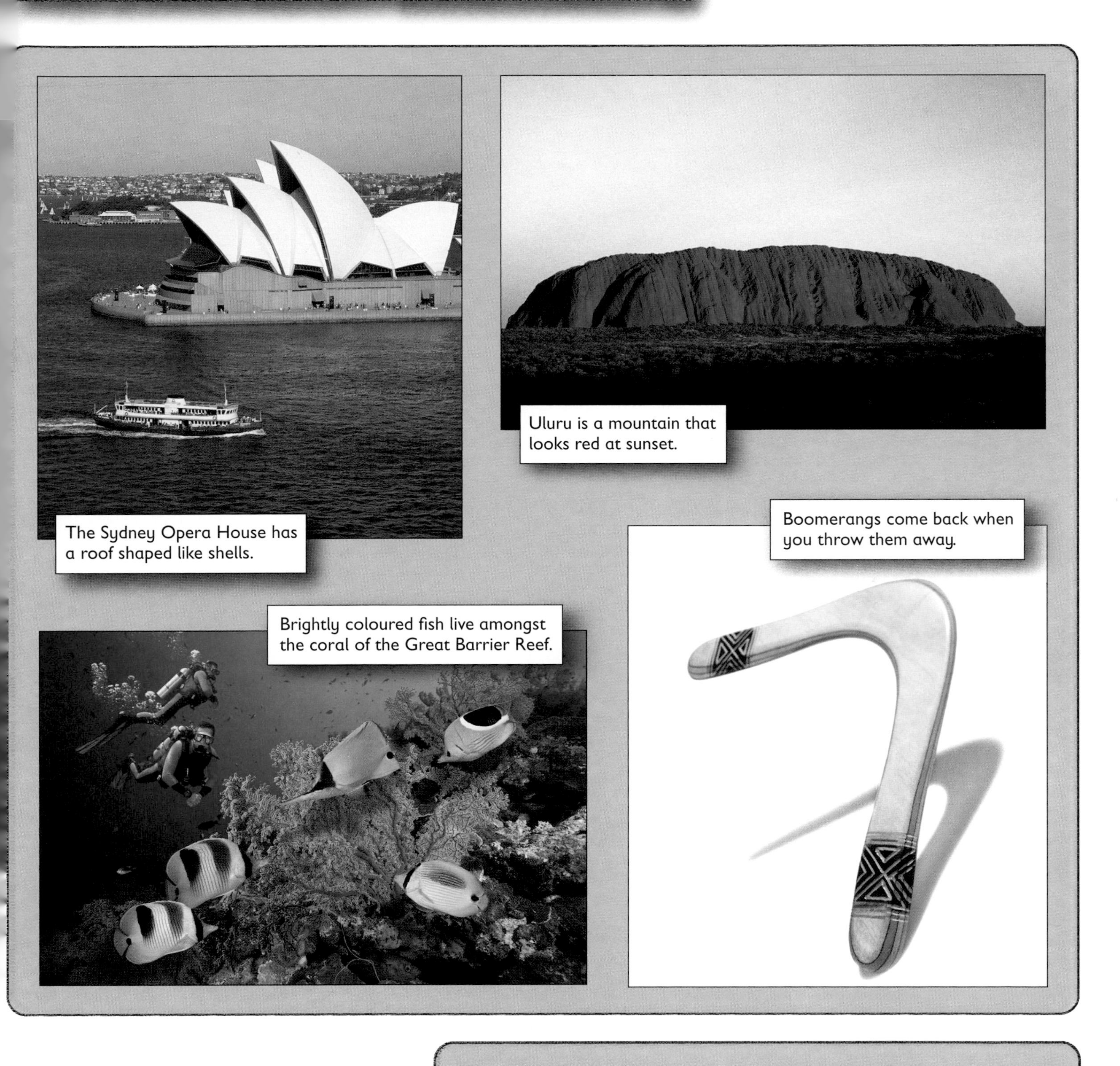

The Sydney Opera House has a roof shaped like shells.

Uluru is a mountain that looks red at sunset.

Boomerangs come back when you throw them away.

Brightly coloured fish live amongst the coral of the Great Barrier Reef.

There are many islands in Oceania. Can you name some of them?

Antarctica

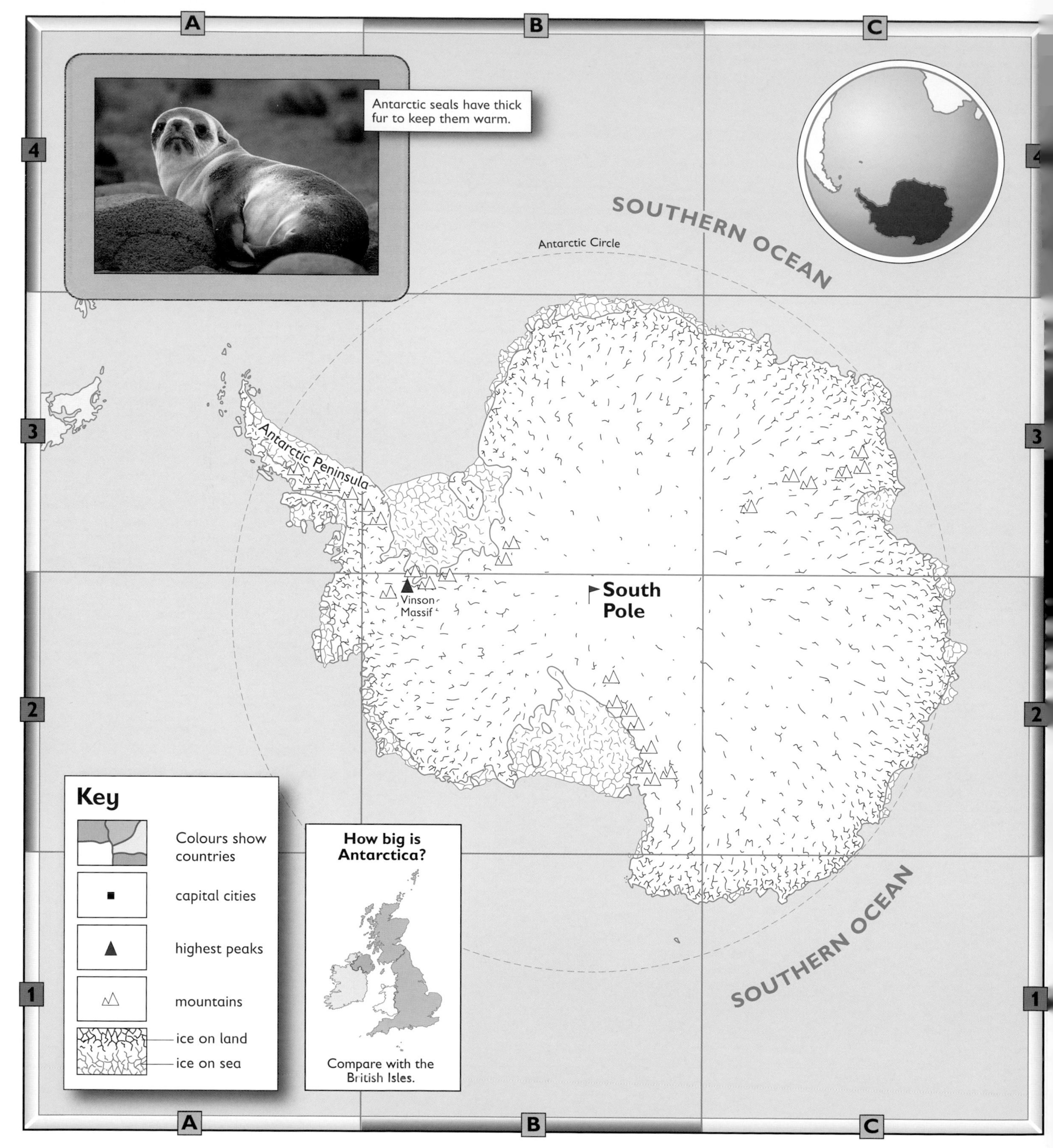

Zenithal Equidistant Projection

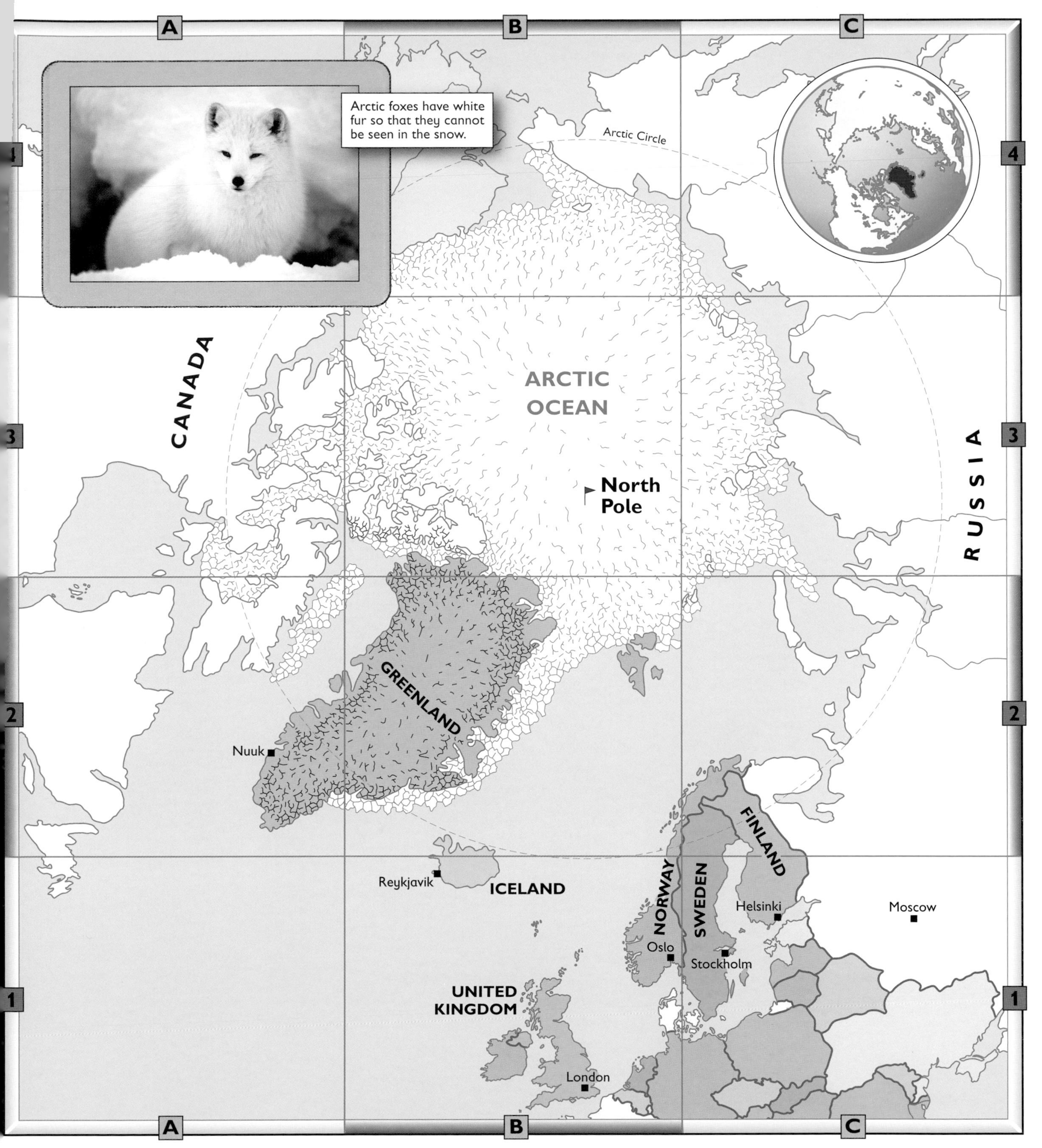
A
B
C
4
3
2
1
Arctic foxes have white fur so that they cannot be seen in the snow.
Arctic Circle
CANADA
ARCTIC OCEAN
North Pole
RUSSIA
GREENLAND
Nuuk
Reykjavik
ICELAND
NORWAY
SWEDEN
FINLAND
Helsinki
Moscow
Oslo
Stockholm
UNITED KINGDOM
London

Index

A list of some of the most important places in this atlas.

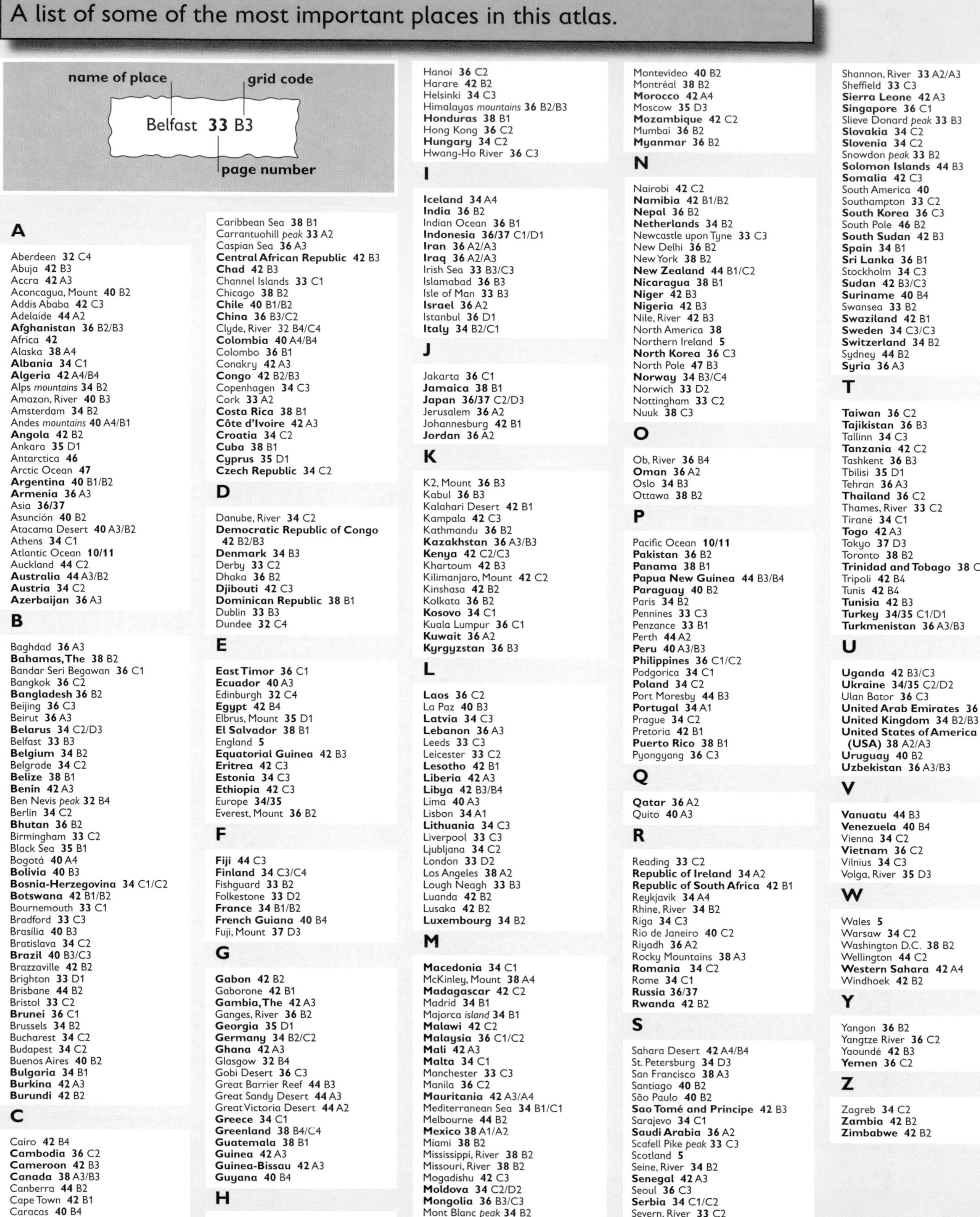

World Flags

Afghanistan | Albania | Algeria | Andorra | Angola | Antigua and Barbuda | Argentina

Armenia | Australia | Austria | Azerbaijan | Bahamas | Bahrain | Bangladesh

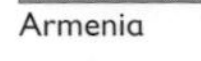 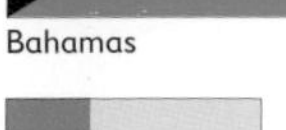  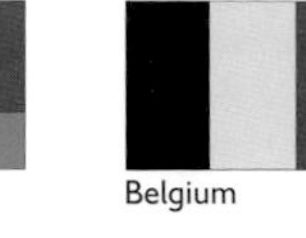  

Barbados | Belarus | Belgium | Belize | Benin | Bhutan | Bolivia

 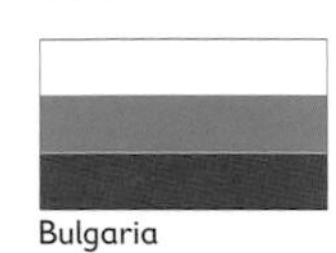  

Bosnia-Herzegovina | Botswana | Brazil | Brunei | Bulgaria | Burkina | Burundi

Cambodia | Cameroon | Canada | Cape Verde | Central African Republic | Chad | Chile

China | Colombia | Comoros | Congo | Congo, Dem. Rep. | Costa Rica | Côte d'Ivoire

Croatia | Cuba | Cyprus | Czech Republic | Denmark | Djibouti | Dominica

Dominican Republic | East Timor | Ecuador | Egypt | El Salvador | Equatorial Guinea | Eritrea

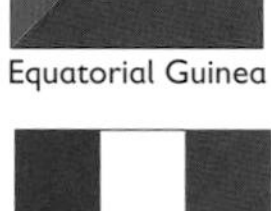    

Estonia | Ethiopia | Fiji | Finland | France | French Guiana | Gabon

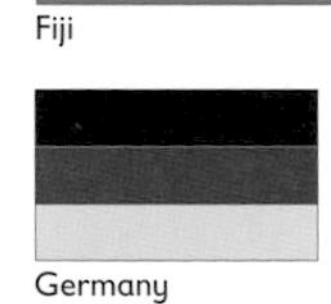  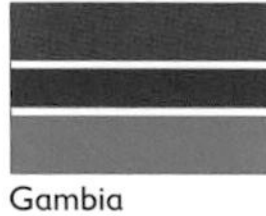  

Gambia | Georgia | Germany | Ghana | Greece | Greenland | Grenada

Guatemala | Guinea | Guinea-Bissau | Guyana | Haiti | Honduras | Hungary

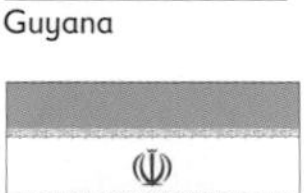    

Iceland | India | Indonesia | Iran | Iraq | Ireland | Israel

     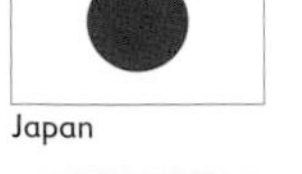

Italy | Jamaica | Japan | Jordan | Kazakhstan | Kenya | Kiribati

    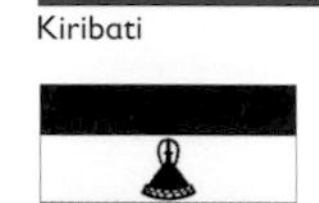

Kosovo | Kuwait | Kyrgyzstan | Laos | Latvia | Lebanon | Lesotho

FINCHES
AND THEIR CARE
TS-107

Photographers: Dr. Herbert R. Axelrod, Joshua Charap and Herschel Frey, Terry Dunham, Michael Gilroy, Paul Kwast, Harry V. Lacey, Dan Martin, Midori Shobo, Ron and Val Moat, Klaus Paysan, Heinz Schrempp, William A. Starika, Tierfreunde, Vogelpark Walsrode, Dr. Matthew M. Vriends.

Distributed in the UNITED STATES by T.F.H. Publications, Inc., One T.F.H. Plaza, Neptune City, NJ 07753; in CANADA to the Pet Trade by H & L Pet Supplies Inc., 27 Kingston Crescent, Kitchener, Ontario N2B 2T6; Rolf C. Hagen Ltd., 3225 Sartelon Street, Montreal 382 Quebec; in CANADA to the Book Trade by Macmillan of Canada (A Division of Canada Publishing Corporation), 164 Commander Boulevard, Agincourt, Ontario M1S 3C7; in ENGLAND by T.F.H. Publications Limited, Cliveden House/Priors Way/Bray, Maidenhead, Berkshire SL6 2HP, England; in AUSTRALIA AND THE SOUTH PACIFIC by T.F.H. (Australia) Pty. Ltd., Box 149, Brookvale 2100 N.S.W., Australia; in NEW ZEALAND by Ross Haines & Son, Ltd., 82 D Elizabeth Knox Place, Panmure, Auckland, New Zealand; in the PHILIPPINES by Bio-Research, 5 Lippay Street, San Lorenzo Village, Makati Rizal; in SOUTH AFRICA by Multipet Pty. Ltd., Box 235 New Germany, South Africa 3620. Published by T.F.H. Publications, Inc. Manufactured in the United States of America by T.F.H. Publications, Inc.

FINCHES AND THEIR CARE

CARL ASCHENBORN

Translated by Howard Hirschhorn

A Cut-throat Finch, *Amadina fasciata*. The wide variety of finches makes it possible for almost anyone to find a bird that suits his fancy.

Contents

THE CAGE, BIRDROOM AND AVIARY

"What should a suitable cage look like? It should have a straight, simple design without any ornamentation; most of all it should be easy to clean and should have a cage-box which is high enough and easy to close."

It is not true that estrildid finches need small cages because of their small size. On the contrary, because of their mobility, they require quite roomy houses. This is why a cage for a pair of birds of even the smallest breeds should have a minimum length of 70 cm, a width of about 35 cm and a height of about 40 cm. The space between each wire of a wire cage is also important. For the smallest breeds, it should not be more than 10 mm; 12 mm is a good size for the larger breeds. Keep this in mind when buying a cage, since having too much space between the cage wires can result in injuries to the birds.

Other requirements should also be kept in mind, so you should rely on the expert advice of your pet dealer about which cage to buy. What should a suitable cage look like? It should have a straight, simple design without any ornamentation; most of all it should be easy to clean and should have a cage-box which is high enough and easy to close. Cage-boxes made of sturdy sheet zinc are suitable. Baths made out of plastic are even better. Frequently I have had trouble with light metal boxes which rusted and even became porous after a relatively short time because of the caustic effect of bird droppings and water. Boxes made entirely of wood are not recommended, since even with the greatest care, they rot sooner or later.

A sufficiently large door which closes well and can be locked or which closes by itself (trap door or spring door) is important. Larger cages should have several doors, which allow you to reach into every part of the cage without disturbing its occupants too much. Estrildid finches are generally kept in cages with wire on all sides. These cages are made entirely of metal, tin-plated wire or of wood with bars. The all-metal cage is the most suitable type, because it is the easiest to keep clean. Unpainted bars can be coated with black iron lacquer. This prevents rust or oxidation and improves the appearance of the cage.

An Aurora Finch on a perch stand. Various types of perches and stands are available at your local pet shop.

No matter what type of finch you plan to keep, proper housing is an absolute necessity. Different finch species have different requirements. For instance, the Star Finch may require a nesting box inside its regular cage in order to breed satisfactorily.

A young Gouldian Finch. This youngster still bears its juvenile plumage. In addition, the light-reflecting gape tubercles are still visible on the side of the beak. These tubercles help the parent birds find the beak when feeding time rolls around.

". . . most importantly, the birds are just as happy in a 'simple' metal cage without artificial light but with natural sunlight."

A pair of Red-cheeked Cordonbleus. Under no circumstances may finches be crowded into a cage that is too small. Before purchasing either the cage or the birds, be sure to find out the space requirements for each species you plan to keep.

The visibility into the cage is also better than if the wire is uncoated. Glass cages of various types, known as bird show cases, have also been available in the last few years, as well as combinations of box and glass cages, with and without inside illumination. Such cages, made of walnut, teak or precious woods and blending in with the decor of the living room furniture, are even custom-built to customer specifications. Of course, these cages are very expensive and not every fancier can afford such a domicile for his birds. Do not worry, however, as such cages are not the greatest, no matter how beautiful they look—and most importantly, the birds are just as happy in a "simple" metal cage without artificial light but with natural sunlight. Some of the fancy

A wide variety of products for your finches is available at your local pet shop. The dealer will help you choose the right products for your particular birds.

glass cages feature special glass which can absorb the ultraviolet rays of the sun.

A box-cage with wire only in the front is best suited for breeding single estrildid finch pairs. This type of cage can also be used for acclimatizing sick birds. It provides protection from disturbance as well as drafts. The wooden box-cage should not have rough edges that can become a breeding ground for pests and make the birds very uncomfortable. Caulk over any cracks with putty.

Now a few comments about painting the cages. The color of paint you wish to use is, of course, a matter of taste. One fancier prefers the natural color of the cage wood and uses a high-quality, quick-drying varnish which can be tinted to match the color of the other furniture in the room. Another fancier likes green or white cages. Any zinc oxide paint can be used; however, you should not use any leaded paint or nitro paint. A light paint is recommended for the inside of the cage, since the birds show up better against it as contrasted to a dark background. A light yellow (ivory-colored) or completely light green shade is better than an all-white paint.

Now some comments on the inside equipment of cages. The perches should be made of soft wood, should not be too thick and should have various widths. Arrange them in such a manner so that the lower perches cannot be soiled by birds sitting on the upper perches. In a smaller cage, place the perches directly under each other. In a large flight cage, position the perches like a flight of stairs, leaving enough horizontal space between each perch.

Many fanciers prefer natural branches over store-bought perches. In the larger flight cage, natural branches certainly look nicer than the uniform-shaped purchased perches and are undoubtedly more pleasing to the birds. Branches of

"The color of paint you wish to use is, of course, a matter of taste. One fancier prefers the natural color of the cage wood . . . Another fancier likes green or white cages."

An Australian Zebra Finch in flight.

Bast: a strong woody fiber, made from the sieve tubes and cells of plants, that is often used in matting, weaving, and fabrics.

An Aurora Finch.

various bushes as well as willow or birch branches are suitable. Make sure that the flight area is not narrowed too much by too many perches. Leave an area in the middle of the cage free for the unhindered flight of the birds. With estrildid finches, providing sleeping boxes, which many species like to use for overnighting, is important. Cone, pear or pipe-shaped "sleeping nests" made of woven bast and cane, open on one side or having an opening in the front, can be obtained at the pet shop. Also available are smaller wooden boxes which have an opening in the front.

You yourself can pad these sleeping nests with bast fibers, blades of grass, etc., or let the birds do it by leaving these materials in the cage. Place the sleeping nests in

A pair of Blue-capped Cordonbleus. This species has a narrow range in eastern Africa.

A Crimson Finch. The Crimson Finch is also known as the Australian Firefinch or the Blood Finch.

the top third areas of the cage. With smaller cages, put them on the outside of the cage to provide more room inside the cage.

The location of the cage is important for the well-being of the birds. They need light and air. This is why the cage should be located near a window. Make sure, however, that it does not get any draft. The birds also need the sun. This is why rooms facing north (in the northern hemisphere) are less suitable for bird keeping and require special lighting. The birds must not be exposed to the full glare of the sun without protection. Partly covering the cage gives them the chance to find a shady spot. Finally, the cage should be hung on or attached to the wall at eye level, so that the birds can be easily observed. In addition, the

Dybowski's Twinspot on a natural branch. Pet shops often sell safe natural branches.

Orange-cheeked Waxbill (lower branch), Red-billed Firefinches (outer birds), and Bronze Mannikins (inner birds). Make sure that the species you plan to keep are compatible before you put them in the same aviary.

"The location of the cage is important for the well-being of the birds. They need light and air. This is why the cage should be located near a window."

A pair of Long-tailed Grassfinches. Birds prefer natural branches, as they can change the size of their grip, thus exercising the muscles of their feet.

birds feel more secure if the cage is positioned in this way as opposed to being placed on a table or low shelf.

What has been said about the small cage also applies generally to the large cage, the community or flight cage in which a large number of estrildid finches are kept together. To make handling easier, the larger cages with floor space should have two or more cage-boxes, each about 40 to 50 cm in width. The community cage should also have several doors, with a large door on the front side allowing easy access for cleaning or bringing tree branches, nesting or sleeping boxes into the cage.

It is the desire of every serious bird fancier to have a birdroom. The novice bird owner is often disappointed when his ideas of the advantages of birdrooms as compared to cages prove to be incorrect.

Setting up a birdroom and keeping the right species of birds in it requires some experience. Not every kind of bird is suitable for the birdroom. There are species which are incompatible with other species or even with their own kind, especially during the incubation period. They disturb the breeding process by destroying the nests of other birds or by destroying eggs and killing chicks. Even among the most peaceful species there are occasionally troublemakers who can completely disrupt the harmony of the birdroom. Conversely, many species will begin breeding only in a birdroom or only in that environment which will display the pleasant sides of their nature and their mobility.

The birdroom must be continually observed. If you have collected a compatible community and removed the troublemakers, you can believe that watching the life and activity in a tastefully appointed birdroom can be a never-ending source of pleasure and stimulation.

A Painted Finch. Finches must never be kept in a birdroom with insufficient warmth, no matter how hardy their particular species is.

Any room which receives sunlight at any time of the day is suitable as a birdroom. The estrildid finches which come to us from warm climates especially need the sun. This is why they should not be kept in a room facing north.

The birdroom should also have heating, since you should not allow those birds that come from the tropics to spend the winter in a cold room. Of course, you should not try to acclimatize them to such conditions, although many estrildid finches are not as sensitive to the cold as one would imagine, considering their origin. A birdroom should have some source of heat, maintaining a temperature of about 15 to 25°C, depending on the species of its occupants. Surround the heating units with wire netting so that the birds, which like to get close to anything giving off heat, cannot burn their feet. Cover the window opening with wire netting in such a way that the window can be opened

"The estrildid finches which come to us from warm climates especially need the sun. This is why they should not be kept in a room facing north."

A Black-headed Munia. It is recommended that munias be kept with species of the same size, as they sometimes bully smaller birds.

or closed. A small platform surrounded by wire netting in front of the window is very useful. This balcony not only enables the birds to take a sun bath, but also gives them a chance to sit in the rain, which a number of birds very much like to do. To improve the air, it is recommended to have some living leaf plants in the room. Philodendrons and ivy are quite suitable for this purpose. Sprinkling these plants with water during the warm season and also during the heating period will insure that the air in the birdroom has the necessary humidity. A small fountain, which is not hard to install, can serve the same purpose. The fountain can also be used by the birds for bathing.

Attach safe branches and bushes to the walls of the birdroom. They are used for perching, and some species also like to build their sometimes very artistic nests in them. Make sure that you leave enough space in the middle of the birdroom to allow unhindered flight of the birds.

It is recommended to set up a feeding table to avoid fighting and to have a place for the feeders and waterers, which should be available in sufficient numbers. Do not wallpaper a birdroom. Remove any previously applied wallpaper when setting up the birdroom for the first time. Whitewash the walls and renew the whitewash at least once a year. Make sure the floor is watertight and sprinkle it with sand. Do not forget to provide a sufficient number of sleeping boxes and nests. They should not, however, be attached to the wall which is farthest from the light. Finally, the birdroom should have illumination, so that the birds can feed during the long winter nights. It is sensible to use lighting with timers which not only turn the lights on and off automatically but are also set for gradual brightening or dimming. The fancier who is the lucky owner of a garden can set up a garden or flight aviary.

I do want to mention specifically that in an aviary you cannot collect all species of estrildid finches indiscriminately. Not all birds are

A variety of dietary supplements for birds are available at your local pet shop.

A pair of adult Red-headed Gouldian Finches.

Species: a taxonomical group of individuals that have common attributes and are capable of interbreeding, designated by a common name and by a binomial consisting of the genus name and a latinized noun or adjective that grammatically agrees with the generic name.

A pair of Painted Finches. Painted Finches are known for their shyness.

peaceful. Some attack each other, particularly during the breeding season, and violent fights—especially between closely related species—are not unusual. This is why it is necessary to familiarize yourself with the living habits of the species you are interested in before buying birds or placing them in the aviary. The extensive literature which is available will help you in this selection, so that you can avoid mistakes in collecting and feeding the birds right from the beginning. It should also be mentioned that you keep estrildid finches in an open flight aviary without any heated shelter *only* between mid-May and late September (in the northern hemisphere), because raw, damp and cold weather is very dangerous for the birds.

If, however, a heated shelter or house is attached to an open flight, you may permit the birds to go into the open flight on dry, sunny, and not too windy winter days, even with frost in the air. The best time is midday, when they can bask in the rays of the winter sun. Of course, make sure the animals spend the nights in the heated shelter or house by closing the small door between the shelter and the open flight. Do not attempt any acclimatization experiments. Keep in mind that most estrildid finches come from tropical areas.

A pair of Melba Finches. Safe, non-toxic plants help improve air quality in the birdroom, and they also add a decorative touch.

An African Silverbill. A well-balanced diet is imperative for the health of your finches. Green food, seed, and animal food must be clean and fresh.

"If . . . a heated shelter or house is attached to an open flight, you may permit the birds to go into the open flight on dry, sunny, and not too windy winter days, even with frost in the air."

FOOD AND FEEDING

"The basis for the successful management of cage birds is the right kind of food."

The basis for the successful management of cage birds is the right kind of food. The well-being and health of the birds, the success of the incubation during breeding, and the growth of the chicks all depend on it. Pay particular attention to the proper condition of the food, i.e. that seed food is fresh. It must be full-grained and dust-free and should not have any damp odor.

Millet is the staple food of the estrildid finches. They also feed on canary seeds, some grass seeds, hemp seeds, shredded oats, etc. There are many kinds of millet which can be used for food. They include large and small-grain varieties such as white millet, silver millet, Plata millet, Japan millet, as well as Senegal millet, mohair millet and finally spray millet, which all

Orange-cheeked Waxbills (outside) and a Black-rumped Waxbill (inside). The Black-rumped Waxbill is also known as the Red-eared Waxbill.

A trio of Long-tailed Grassfinches. If you plan to keep a number of birds, be sure to give a sufficient amount of food. It is also important to see that weaker birds are not kept away from their meals by stronger, more dominant cagemates.

estrildid finches like very much. These birds also like to feed on half-ripe blood millet and bristle millet, which grow as weeds in many regions. The fancier who has a garden should disseminate some millet, since estrildid finches like to feed on half-ripe millet seeds as well as half-ripe grass seeds, needing that food for their own well-being and to rear their young; in their native habitat, they do not feed exclusively on ripe seeds. In winter, you should give the birds not only dry seed food, but also some soaked and sprouting seeds. Soak the seeds in a bowl filled with water and serve them when they begin to sprout. Before serving the seeds, make sure they are clean and allow time for the water to drain off. Green food such as delicate lettuce, spinach and dandelion leaves are important for maintaining health. An even better green food is bird chickweed, which is available throughout the year.

The popular room plant tradescantia, specifically its green-leafed viridis variety, is a useful green food in the winter. All green food must be fresh, not wilted, which can easily happen with lettuce; it must not be given to the birds in a frosted condition, because it can then cause intestinal illnesses.

As do most finches, the estrildid finches supplement their natural diet with all kinds of insects and their

A Red-breasted Bluebill.

Ant pupae: intermediate metamorphic stage of members of the family Formicidae which comes after the larval stage and before sexual maturity.

pupae and small worms. They are the main growing food for the nest chicks.

Along with seed food, this animal food is also important for our birds. The most important animal food is fresh or frozen ant pupae, which should be warmed briefly to prevent the ants from slipping out. If fresh pupae are not available, you can offer dried ant pupae. This food, however, should be soaked in milk, since many estrildid finches will not accept it or will only accept it reluctantly in a dry condition. You can also offer ground, hard-boiled egg yolk. Other suitable foods include breakfast rolls softened in milk, and white bread or zwieback. You should always have an insect food mixture or breeding food on hand. You can find a large number of very good mixtures at the pet shop. Mix the food with cottage cheese or finely grated carrots until it forms a lightly moistened, flaky and crumbly paste. It should be prepared early enough so that the dry portions of the food mixture are soaked before being offered to the birds.

Along with the food mixtures, you should also offer, if available, all kinds of living insects, small worms, all kinds of flies and their mites, including the vinegar fly, the stubby-

winged fruitfly, which can be easily bred, gnat larvae and finally water fleas and tubifex, etc. This food is similar to that used for the aquarium or terrarium.

As we can see, the estrildid finches have an extensive and varied natural food menu. It should be mentioned, however, that the fancier who wants to keep only a pair of birds, or several birds belonging to a less fragile species, and does not intend to breed them, can keep his birds healthy for a long time with normal

A nutritious diet is of the utmost importance in keeping any living creature healthy and happy.

The diet of the Star Finch should be supplemented with spray millet and mealworms, especially during the breeding season.

Cuttlefish bone shell: the internal dorsal shell of the cuttlefish, an important source of calcium for cage birds.

estrildid finch food, millet seeds (obtainable at any pet shop), and some green food.

When buying the food, keep in mind that it should be suitable for the birds. For example, it should contain enough small-grained millet for the astrilds with fine tapered beaks, whereas the amadines, birds with thick beaks, prefer large-grained millet. You should buy bird food in a pet shop, not at the market.

Remember that finches also need calcium. There are a number of calcium supplements that can be purchased at pet shops. You can also give the birds finely ground egg shells or fine oystershell grit or even the well-known cuttlefish bone shell.

Various containers can be used as feeding dishes. Made of glass, porcelain, stoneware or plastic, they can be purchased in all shapes and forms. There are also automatic feeders and waterers. An automatic feeding device is recommended for a larger flight containing a larger number of birds.

An automatic feeding box with a shell collector has a number of advantages over the normal feeders. It stores a larger amount of food, requiring less frequent refilling. The food remains free of shells, since during feeding they fall into the shell collector. From the collector, they pass into a drawer which can be emptied as required. This automatic feeder also prevents food waste. It can be bought in pet shops.

If you use automatic waterers, you must then be sure to offer separate baths. These come in all shapes and sizes. In the birdroom or aviary, you can use any glass, porcelain,

Note the open beaks of these young Society Finches as the parent bird comes in for a landing.

"Ever since I started keeping birds, I have always used the simple stoneware flowerpot saucers which have been accepted by the birds because of their subdued color."

stoneware or plastic dish. Ever since I started keeping birds, I have always used the simple stoneware flowerpot saucers which have been accepted by the birds because of their subdued color. Make sure that the water in the baths is not deeper than two centimeters. If you also keep birds which are larger than the estrildid finches, whose baths have to be deeper, lay a tight-fitting stone in the bath to make bathing easier for the small estrildid finches.

A Swee Waxbill. This bird is also known as Dufresne's Waxbill.

BREEDING

"The fancier who wants to breed estrildid finches should not only have some experience in management and care of these birds, but should also have learned a great deal about their habits. . ."

The fancier who wants to breed estrildid finches should not only have some experience in management and care of these birds, but should also have learned a great deal about their habits; just because one or another novice estrildid finch fancier was immediately successful in breeding a pair of these small exotic birds without difficulty does not prove that they are easy to breed. In general, breeding estrildid finches, especially the small astrilds, is not so easy. There are a number of factors which can thwart successful breeding and the fledging of the chicks.

With some species, the difficulties

A pair of Swee Waxbills.

A pair of (Red) Avadavats. Breeding finches is not always easy. Proper conditions are necessary, as are compatible partners and cagemates.

Artist's rendering of a pair of Painted Finches. The male is the upper bird, while the female is the lower.

Clutch: a nest of eggs, comparable to a litter of dogs.

begin when you try to bring the right pairs together. With many birds, both sexes have the same coloring, both sing and two birds of the same sex behave like birds of opposite sexes. It is true that the cock, as a rule, displays unique courtship behavior as he sings; however, the question as to whether you have a pair before you or not is still unanswered. Sometimes after weeks or even months, the bird thought to be a hen reveals itself, by suddenly singing, to be a cock, meaning that breeding is impossible.

Restlessness and anxiety prevent many birds from breeding. The slightest disturbance causes them to abandon their clutch and chicks. Others build their nests regularly and lay eggs but do not incubate them, leaving the nest and eggs to begin the whole process again somewhere else. This behavior indicates that their breeding drive is too strong. It can happen that the chicks are incubated, but are not fed at all or are abandoned after several days for no obvious reason. When this occurs, something is probably missing in the food or surroundings. Some birds breed without hesitation in a cage; others need a large room all to themselves. In flight aviaries, a sudden change in the weather can cause the incubation to fail. In many cases, having too many birds in the breeding area is responsible for the failure. Keep in mind that some species are vicious to their own or to closely related species, especially during the breeding season, so that only one pair can be kept in the aviary. Finally, there are species which are incorrigible troublemakers, which not only destroy the nests of their fellow inhabitants, but also throw out their eggs and small nest chicks.

Conversely, there are species which take easily to breeding, producing one successful incubation after another, regardless of the time of year. The Society Finch, a cultivated bird bred long ago by the Japanese, probably from a Bronze Mannikin species, is one of these birds. Another easy-to-breed species is the white variety bred by the Chinese from the blue Java Sparrow. Both of these birds are domesticated animals. Another easy-to-breed species is the Australian Zebra Finch. It is already domesticated, breeds easily, incubates reliably and rears its young safely. The Society Finch is of value to the estrildid

A pair of Long-tailed Grassfinches. The sexes in this species are very much alike, although the female usually has a smaller, narrower throat patch.

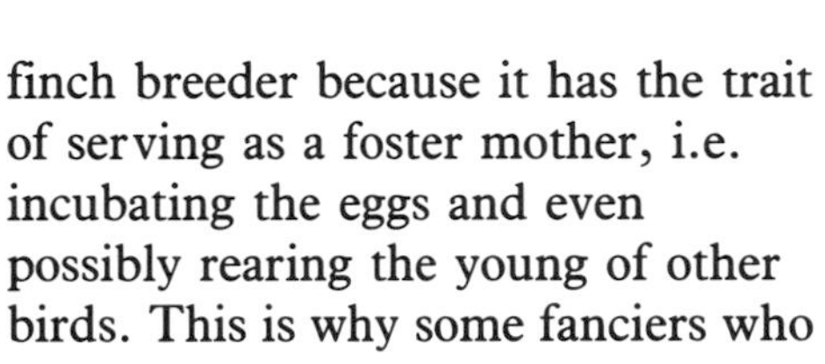

finch breeder because it has the trait of serving as a foster mother, i.e. incubating the eggs and even possibly rearing the young of other birds. This is why some fanciers who

"The Society Finch is of value to the estrildid finch breeder because it has the trait of serving as a foster mother, i.e. incubating the eggs and even possibly rearing the young of other birds."

A trio of Peter's Twinspots. This particular species has been bred in captivity many times, but it does not like to have its nest checked.

A White headed Munia.

own especially valuable estrildid finches which do not incubate reliably keep a pair or several pairs of Society Finches in reserve, so that if required they can incubate the eggs of the other birds. However, the eggs of the Society Finches must be removed. If left to incubate their own eggs and eggs of other birds at the same time, there is the danger that they will give preference to their own young. Most estrildid finch breeders today try to do without Society Finches, because some of their traits are passed on to the young birds and the reproductive ability of the valuable and rare estrildid finches diminishes from generation to generation. Make sure

Incubation: the act of keeping the clutch of eggs warm by sitting on them, performed by one or both of the parent birds.

A Chestnut Munia, *Lonchura malacca ferruginosa*. This race is often called the Black-throated Munia.

that the eggs of the foster mother's birds are not older than the eggs of the other birds to be incubated. A time difference of one to two days is not significant. If you want the Society Finches to rear other bird's chicks, the best time for that is when the chicks have hatched. At that time, they will be most readily accepted by the fostering birds. Nine-day-old birds will most likely not be accepted.

The sleeping boxes previously mentioned can also be used as nesting boxes if they have a space of 12 x 12 cm and a height of 12–14 cm. They are, however, too small for the species which build large nests. The usual budgerigar boxes are used by large species for building nests. Remove the perches, feeders and waterers and the bars on the narrow side of the cage and cover the remaining sides with cardboard, wood or canvas. Nesting boxes should be available in sufficient numbers—one or two for each pair of birds—to avoid fights caused by the scarcity of nesting space. Some species, even in captivity, build only free-standing nests. Make sure that enough branches or twigs are on hand for the birds to build their frequently very artistic nests. Bundles or reeds piled up vertically are useful for this purpose.

Various materials such as coconut and sisal fibers (about ten centimeters long), blades of straw or grass and bast can be used for nest-

Many finches will hybridize with other species. This particular bird is a Society Finch hybrid, probably a silverbill cross.

"Nesting boxes should be available in sufficient numbers—one or two for each pair of birds—to avoid fights caused by the scarcity of nesting space."

A pair of Swee Waxbills. Purebred birds are usually more beautiful than hybrids, and most experienced breeders would advise novices not to crossbreed.

building. The birds take special care in building the inside of their nest. They use animal and plant wool, feathers, moss, etc., for that purpose. The often large nests require a suitably large amount of nesting materials. Make sure that these materials are available in sufficient amounts and variety. Also keep in mind that if the materials run out, the birds might steal them from other nests to use in building their own.

The basic principle applying to rearing food is that it should be both nutritious and varied. Some reject ant pupae and want only breakfast rolls soaked in milk or white bread, whereas others want only ant pupae

A pair of White-headed Munias in the nest. Some species will take longer than others to settle down and breed.

A pair of Star Finches.

Rearing food: special food that is given to incubating parent birds and later to young birds, often includes insects and soaked bread.

Inbreeding: the act of crossing closely related animals such as fathers and daughters, concentrating both good and bad genetic traits in the young produced.

when rearing their young. Sometime before the onset of incubation, introduce soft food; do not wait until the young are hatched. This will allow you to find out what the individual pairs prefer.

Once the chicks can feed themselves, take them out of the breeding room, because they often disturb the next incubation of their parents or are bothered by their parents.

Finally, the novice should not begin by breeding the difficult or expensive species, but rather should gain his first breeding experience by trying his hand with Society Finches or Zebra Finches. This way, you can avoid much disappointment. When breeding these species, guard against too much inbreeding. Do not cross fathers with daughters, mothers with sons, or brothers with sisters throughout entire generations. The inevitable result of this inbreeding is the continually increasing degeneration of the offspring. Insure that new blood is regularly introduced into the breeding stock by buying several cocks and hens at the pet shop or by swapping birds with another breeder.

In closing this chapter, I would like to touch briefly on hybrid breeding, i.e. crossing members of varying categories and species. Especially with estrildid finches, many mixed breeds have been produced, not by crossing closely related animals, but rather by crossing birds of largely non-related species. In most cases, this mixed breeding happened not by plan, but by accident.

Every birdroom, aviary or community cage will have a single

A pair of White-headed Munias. These birds are often called White-headed Nuns.

An array of nesting boxes. Your pet dealer can help you choose the proper type of nest for the species you wish to breed.

bird which has lost its partner of the same species or for which a partner—usually a hen—cannot be obtained at the bird supplier. These lone birds, having the strongly developed social instinct of the estrildid finches, will team up with some single member of another species which is in the same situation and will sometimes begin breeding with this substitute partner. The products of these "mixed marriages" can be quite interesting hybrids which, following the laws of heredity, can resemble in plumage coloring and nature one or the other parent bird or can possess traits of both parents. Mostly, they do not attain the beauty of their parents, not having the pure plumage color of their forebears, and are regarded by and large as curiosities. Three-way marriages also occur sometimes. Once I had a pair of old bright yellow Society Finches with which I discovered, after incubation, a weird-looking chick. In both plumage and figure, it resembled an African Silverbill and also had its lead-gray beak. The father of this hybrid was obviously a lone African Silverbill cock, often occupying the same nest as the Society Finches, which had "seduced" the Society Finch hen in an opportune moment.

Hybrid breeding, however, can also be carried out intentionally, perhaps to enjoy rare, previously not produced mixed breeds. It can also be done to preserve a species which is no longer available, because of an export embargo, when only one partner is present and it is bred with a closely related species to produce mixed breeds. This reverse breeding is continued until, gradually, birds which closely resemble the species you are trying to preserve evolve (displacement breeding). Finally, producing mixed breeds can also be helpful to science by giving it the opportunity, through varying fertility of the hybrids, to determine the degree of affinity of the parent birds, so that their place in the total bird classification system can be established.

Hybrid breeding: cross-breeding between birds of different species or subspecies, often carried out in captivity and occasionally occurring in nature where the territories of similar animals overlap.

ILLNESS

Hospital cage: a separate cage in which a single bird can be quarantined upon arrival or upon showing signs of illness, usually containing a heat lamp to keep the bird warm.

It has already been mentioned that estrildid finches are often quite feeble when they arrive upon our shores and must be carefully acclimatized. Once acclimatized, they prove to be modest and steadfast, and, with the proper management and care, show no more susceptibility to sickness than other species of birds. The most difficult aspect of an illness is the diagnosis, i.e. correctly identifying it. Often the experienced bird fancier will be able to recognize an illness by observing its symptoms, as for example, with a cold, and be able to apply the proper remedy. Conversely, the novice fancier will not be able, most of the time, to find the cause of the most recognizable illness. Often he makes the basic mistake of initiating treatment, causing the death of a bird which could have been cured with the proper procedure. When a bird becomes sick, the first thing that should be done is to isolate it in a hospital cage by itself. This prevents the other birds from becoming infected and provides the sick bird the necessary rest and additional heat lamp warmth. Treatment, as recommended by a veterinarian, can begin only after the patient has been isolated in a hospital cage.

A Black-rumped Waxbill. A healthy finch will have bright eyes, clean plumage, and an active interest in its surroundings.

A lovely Gold-breasted Waxbill.

A pair of Australian Zebra Finches, a fawn cock and a normal hen.

A pied cock Zebra Finch.

The Australian Zebra Finch is one of the most commonly kept species in the world.

THE INDIVIDUAL SPECIES

"To provide the reader with the most vivid picture of the individual species, making it possible for him to identify the species, I have described the plumage coloring in detail."

I would like to point out that the limited scope of this small book has unfortunately prevented me from presenting in words and pictures all the imported estrildid finches. Nevertheless, I have included not only the most common birds available on the market—well-known species—but have also described a number of rarer species, especially the new introductions of the last few years, to give the fancier the widest possible perspective of the total range of these birds.

To provide the reader with the most vivid picture of the individual species, making it possible for him to identify the species, I have described the plumage coloring in detail. I have also included details on size in centimeters, measured usually from the tip of the beak over the back to the tip of the tail. Experience shows, however, that measuring the total length is not accurate. Especially regarding estrildid finches, these measurements give a totally incorrect impression of the actual size of these miniature birds. Determining the body weight does not help because, compared to the Little Winter Gold Cock, having a total length of not quite nine centimeters and weighing four to six grams, a member of the smallest estrildid finch species of the same length and of about the same weight looks astonishingly small. The solution to this puzzle of differing size despite the same length and weight is the different thickness of the plumage and, above all, the varying length of the feathers.

I would like to begin with two species which have not at all or have only rarely been imported and which, as almost exclusively insect-eaters, differ in eating habits from all other estrildid finches. The first of these species, *Parmoptila*, consists of only one type, the Antpecker *(Parmoptila woodhousei)* from the forests of west and central Africa, where it can be found in four different varieties; the second group, the Blacklings *(Nigrita)*, distributed in the same area and in a few bordering mountain forest regions of east Africa, consists of four types. The three types of Shelley's Olivebacks *(Nesocharis)* resemble in some aspects the Blacklings and also have some similarity to the green

A Yellow-winged Pytilia.

A lovely Cut-throat Finch. This species is relatively easy to find on the bird market, whereas other species will vary from common to almost impossible to locate.

Savannah: a tropical or sub-tropical grassy terrain which contains some scattered trees and drought-resistant undergrowth.

astrilds. These birds are very difficult to acclimatize. They inhabit forest fringes and mountain forest areas of west and central Africa. Their plumage shows mainly blue-gray, gold-green, yellow and white colors.

The Melba Finch, *Pytilia melba*, inhabiting the savannah and brierbush areas of Africa from Senegal and Sudan to Namibia, Transvaal and Natal, in numerous races of various colors, is one of the most beautiful astrilds (estrildid finches with fine-tapered beaks). The Melba Finch hen does not have the red markings on the head and throat; with the hen, these parts are colored gray. The Melba Finch has a length of 12–13 cm. Its song is made up of whistling, gurgling and trilling sounds which can vary, depending on the race. In captivity, Melba Finches need much light and warmth (at least 20°C). For food, they need both seed food (Senegal millet, canary seed) and plenty of animal food (when possible ant pupae, otherwise or additionally egg food, soft food, no flour worms), which is essential for rearing the young. These birds were bred successfully for the first time in 1963 by K. Koenig. Melba Finches are not compatible with birds of their own species and other *Pytilia* types. Also be careful when keeping them with other estrildid finches in a small room.

The following races of the Melba Finch are occasionally imported: the Damara Melba Finch, *Pytilia melba damarensis,* from south and central Angola, Namibia and south Zambia to Zimbabwe and Transvaal; the Natal Melba Finch, *Pytilia melba thamnophila,* from Natal and south Mozambique; the Grot Melba Finch, *Pytilia melba grotei,* from the coastal areas of east Africa from the Zambesi to north Tanzania; the Kenya Melba Finch, *Pytilia melba percivali,* from central Kenya and north Tanzania, the most available bird on the market; the Eritrea Melba Finch, *Pytilia melba jessei,* from Eritrea; Kirk's Melba Finch, *Pytilia melba kirki,* from the coastal area of Kenya; and finally the Yellow-throated Melba Finch, *Pytilia*

A pair of Melba Finches. Melba Finches come in a variety of races (or subfamilies), and they are occasionally available for sale.

melba citerior, from Senegal to northern Sudan. Besides these races, there are six or seven distinguishable races, including the *Pytilia melba melba* race from the coastal area of north Angola, which have been imported in a living condition.

The 12 cm long Orange-winged Pytilia, *Pytilia afra*, from eastern Africa to Angola and north Transvaal, is related to the Melba Finch. Plumage coloring of the cock: headmask red; back crown blue-gray; back and wings gold-olive; flight feathers edged in orange-yellow on the outside; upper tail coverts and mid-tail feathers red; underside olive-brown with fine yellowy-white diagonal stripes; middle of the stomach whitish; eye and beak red; feet flesh-colored. The hen does not have the red headmask. The Orange-winged Pytilia is more robust than the Melba Finch but also needs, along with the Melba Finch, much warmth and animal food. It is not quite as quarrelsome as its relative. It breeds easily and reliably and, when rearing, needs fresh ant pupae as well as plant lice. Mixed breeds have been reared with Aurora Finch hens; Orange-winged Pytilias owned by Frhr. v. Kittlitz-Ottendorf reared Paradise Whydahs. In the wild, they are parasitized by the Broadtail Paradise Whydahs, which lay their eggs in the Orange-wing nests.

The Aurora Finch, *Pytilia phoenicoptera*, which is found in several races from Gambia to Ethiopia, is a close relative of the above two astrilds. The Actual Aurora Finch, *Pytilia phoenicoptera phoenicoptera*, inhabits Gambia to northern Nigeria, whereas the Stripe Finch, *Pytilia phoenicoptera lineata*, is found in Ethiopia. The Aurora Finch has a length of about 11-13 cm. The quite attractive coloring of the cock: head, upperside gray; back faded reddish; wing coverts reddish; underside light gray-white ribboned;

An Orange-winged Pytilia. This species is a reliable breeder, and it has been hybridized with the Aurora Finch.

flight feathers dark gray-brown with broad, bright crimson red edges; tail black-brown; middle feathers and outside vanes of the remaining feathers and upper tail coverts crimson red; eye red; beak black. The Stripe Finch has a red beak; feet reddish-gray. The hen is colored more brownish-gray. The Aurora Finch is imported more frequently, is more robust and less quarrelsome and also needs additional animal food. Breeding succeeds relatively easily with fresh ant pupae. Mixed breeds have been reared with Orange-winged Pytilias.

G. Eckl described breeding the rarely imported Yellow-winged Pytilia, *Pytilia hypogrammica*. This estrildid finch, inhabiting west Africa from Sierra Leone up to the Ubangi-Schari area, looks like an Aurora Finch with the red headmask and the orange-yellow flight feathers of the Orange-winged Pytilia.

The Brown Twinspot, *Clytospiza monteiri*, from Cameroon and north Angola to Uganda, has been rarely imported in the past and has not

Race: alternative term for subspecies, a taxonomical division which ranks below species, specifying that the members of various subspecies have some physical differences but can interbreed successfully, especially where their ranges overlap.

A pair of Melba Finches.

A pair of Orange-winged Pytilias.

been bred. According to J. Nicolai, this bird can be best kept in an aviary with a large amount of plants, where it likes to stay in thick bushes and on the earth floor, hopping around in great leaps.

Imported for the first time in 1961, Dybowski's Twinspot or Dybowski Finch, *Euschistospiza dybowskii*, which lives in Sierra Leone and from Cameroon to southwest Sudan, is somewhat smaller but longer tailed than the Aurora Finch. Plumage coloring of the cock: head, neck and frontal breast shale-gray; back, wings and the long upper tail coverts red; tail feathers black; body underside black, numerous white dots on the flanks; eye dark with a red lid rim; beak black; feet black-brown. The hen has a dark shale-gray, white-dotted underbody. It eats grass seeds as well as insects. It is interesting to note that, according to E. Geiger, the cock he kept was a great joker; it produced the sounds of "the blackbird, the lark and the most splendid trills of a very good singing canary . . . as well as many less known tunes." The bird also answered with the same melodies which were whistled to it. W. Kujawa reported the first breeding of Dybowski's Twinspot. Since then, this bird has been bred repeatedly.

Also imported for the first time a few years ago, the Dusky Twinspot, *Euchistospiza cinereovinacea*, is from Angola and Zaire. Length about 12 cm. The cock's plumage: head and neck dusky gray; back and wings brownish-dusky gray; upper and lower tail coverts dark red; tail

". . .[The Brown Twinspot] can best be kept in an aviary with a large amount of plants, where it likes to stay in thick bushes and on the earth floor, hopping around in great leaps."

A pair of Aurora Finches, *Pytilia poenicoptera*. Aurora Finches are more commonly imported and are less quarrelsome than birds of other *Pytilia* species.

"With a length of 10-11 cm, the Green Twinspot is initially a quite fragile, not easy-to-keep bird, which needs the most careful acclimatization with warmth and plenty of additional animal food."

black; underside of the body black; sides of the body and breast dark red with a few white drop spots; eye yellowish-brown with a reddish lid rim; beak black; the feet black-brown. The hen is basically the same as the cock, except that its black plumage parts are more gray and it has more drop spots.

The Green Twinspot, *Mandingoa nitidula*, lives in west Africa to Angola, in Zaire and from south Ethiopia to Natal and Transkei. Its west African race, Schlegel's Green Twinspot, *Mandingoa nitidula schlegeli*, was in the past one of the greatest rarities, but has been imported more frequently since 1953. With a length of 10-11 cm, the Green Twinspot is initially a quite fragile, not easy-to-keep bird, which needs the most careful acclimatization with warmth and plenty of additional animal food. F. Karl succeeded in breeding these birds, specifically the *schlegeli* race of these birds, for the first time in 1960. He is of the opinion that Green Twinspots can prove to be hardy birds after they have been acclimatized. The plumage of the colored-out cock: topside moss-green; rump and upper tail coverts orange-red; flight feathers and tail dark green; eye surroundings, frontal cheek, chin and throat red and breast and throat red or green, depending on the race; underbody black with numerous small white drop spots; eye dark brown; beak black with a red tip; feet flesh colored. The cock's head marking is red. The hen's head marking is brown-yellow with just a hint of red. The races *Mandingoa nitidula chubbi* and *M.n. virens* live in east Africa. The former birds inhabit an area from south Ethiopia to Uganda and have fine-tapered beaks; the cock has a faded orange-red throat; the latter ones inhabit an area from north Tanzania to Swaziland and appear to be a transition race which is related to the South African *M.n. nitidula*, located in Natal and Transkei. The *M.n. virens* race has a close to green and sometimes close to faded orange throat; the cocks of the *M.n. nitidula* race usually have a green throat. In recent times, east African birds have been imported repeatedly.

Of the four types of the Red-faced Crimsonwings, *Cryptospiza*, red and olive or red and gray colored birds inhabiting the high mountain ranges of tropical Africa, three are imported rarely or erratically; the most frequent import is Reichenow's Red-faced Crimsonwing, *Cryptospiza reichenovii*, from the Cameroon Mountains and the mountains of east Africa.

The following two species have unusually thick beaks: firstly the Black-bellied Seedcrackers, *Pyrenestes*, which were previously called Black-bellied Weavers. Since up to now only a few specimens have been inspected by fanciers, I would like to mention only the Crimson Seedcracker, *Pyrenestes sanguineus*,

The Melba Finch is also known as the Green-winged Pytilia and is related to the Orange- and Yellow-winged members of this genus.

A pair of Yellow-winged Pytilias. These birds are red-winged mutations of the actual Yellow-wing.

living in the area from Gambia to the Ivory Coast and the Black-bellied Seedcracker, *Pyrenestes ostrinus*, inhabiting west and central Africa.

Their length is 12 to 14 cm. The cock's plumage: head, neck, breast and upper tail coverts scarlet red; tail dark red; remaining plumage brown (Crimson Seedcracker) or black (Black-bellied Seedcracker); eye with conspicuously white lid rim; beak steely blue; feet brown. The hen is red on the brow, crown, cheeks, throat and upper tail coverts, the remaining plumage is olive-brown; the Crimson Seedcracker hen's plumage is darker than that of the Crimson Seedcracker cock. Corresponding to their concealed way of living in swamp thickets, forest glades, etc., these birds prefer to find dark places in larger cages or aviaries and try to hide themselves. They like to bathe. For food they receive the normal estrildid finch food.

The 13-14 cm long, quite imposing Red-breasted Bluebill, *Spermophaga haematina*, with a similarly thick but differently shaped, somewhat thinner beak, is a member of the *Spermophaga* species. Its habitat is in west Africa up to eastern Zaire, and recently it has been available now and then on the market. The plumage of the cock: upper head, sides of the head, nape of the neck and upperside black; upper tail coverts black, dark red or red, depending on the race; chin, throat, breast and sides of the body shining red; middle of the breast and stomach, lower tail coverts dull black; eye red or brown, bluish lid rim; beak blue with a red tip, feet yellowy-brown. The hen: brow, cheeks dull red; upper tail coverts dark red or red, depending on the race; upperside shale-gray; throat, breast and sides of the body lively red; middle of the breast and stomach as well as the backsides of the body black with round, white double spots. The Red-breasted Bluebill, which is not always peaceful during the breeding season, has a pretty song consisting of long drawn-out flute sounds and trills. It

Brown Twinspot. This species is relatively rare in captivity.

Green Twinspot. This species is also called the Green-backed Twinspot.

"The Red-breasted Bluebill, which is not always peaceful during the breeding season, has a pretty song consisting of long drawn-out flute sounds and trills."

also has the talent of a joker: it emits a creaking and squeaking sound. For food it needs, in addition to Senegal millet, etc., sprouted or soaked seeds (millet, canary seed, oats and wheat), since it apparently does not like larger kernels in an unsprouted condition, despite its thick beak.

A 13 cm long, very rarely imported relative is the Red-headed Bluebill, *Spermophaga ruficapilla*. Of equal size and also colored black-red, it is distributed from north Angola to east Africa. The cock's plumage: head, neck, breast and sides of the body as well as the longer upper tail coverts shining red; the remaining plumage black; the *Spermophaga ruficapilla cana* race living in Usambara has shale-gray plumage; eye dark brown; lid rim pale blue; beak steely blue, on the tip reddish; feet black. The hen is grayer and has white drop spotting on the underside. This finch is an excellent room bird, which can be kept together with small species in a spacious birdroom.

Peter's Twinspot, *Hypargos niveoguttatus*, from east Africa to south Mozambique, is imported quite regularly, but mostly in only a few specimens. In the past, this bird was known simply as the Twinspot. Its length is 12-14 cm. Well acclimatized, this bird can be highly recommended not only because of its attractive plumage color but also because of its steadfast and pleasant nature and friendliness. It is, however, not always compatible. The cock's plumage: upper head, neck ash-gray to gray-brown; back and wings cinnamon-brown; rump, upper tail coverts red; tail feathers black; middle tail feathers faded crimson red; head, sides of the neck, throat and upper breast crimson red; underside black with large white drop spots, especially on the sides; eye dark brown with blue lid rim; beak blue-black; feet shale-gray. The hen: sides of the head gray; chin and throat yellow-brownish; maw and upper breast yellow-brownish or red, depending on the race; underside ash-gray with thin black-edged white drop spots. Breeding, even in the

Dybowski's Twinspot.

". . .[Peter's Twinspot] can be highly recommended not only because of its attractive plumage color but also because of its steadfast and pleasant nature and friendliness."

A Dusky Twinspot. This species comes from Angola and Zaire.

Reichenow's Red-faced Crimsonwing, the most common race of this species in captivity.

cage, has been repeatedly successful. Rearing with fresh ant pupae, egg, soaked millet, flour worms and green food. This bird does not like to have its nest checked.

The Rosy Twinspot, *Hypargos margaritatus*, from south Mozambique to Zululand, is as large as and is very similar to the Peter's Twinspot. The cock's plumage color: upper head brown; sides of the head, throat and upper breast are rose-red and the drop spots on the underside slightly pink; eye dark, lid rim blue; beak shale-blue; feet shale-gray. The hen has gray sides of the head, throat and upper breast and whitish underbody mid-section. This finch comes on the market infrequently and has shown itself in the beginning to be very weak; once acclimatized, however, it does not appear to be more difficult to care for than the closely related Peter's Twinspot. It is more similar to the Red-billed Firefinches than is Peter's Twinspot. Food: Senegal millet, canary seed, good soft food, which is often more pleasing to the birds than seed food, fresh ant pupae, small or fresh-skinned flour worms, green food.

The Red-billed Firefinches, *Lagonosticta*, are very attractively colored small African estrildid finches which have been imported in large numbers and which in the bird trade are often mistaken for other birds. Unfortunately, these pretty, mainly red-colored estrildid finches are quite weak up until total acclimatization; healthy Red-billed Firefinches are, especially when they are kept in pairs, often quite aggressive with their own kind as well as with other *Lagonosticta* species; especially during the breeding season, fights between cocks ending in death can occur. They are mostly peaceful with other estrildid finches. This is why you should keep only a pair of the Red-billed Firefinch species in a birdroom or aviary at any one time.

The Brown-rumped Firefinch or Brown Firefinch, *Lagonosticta nitidula*, has its habitat in Angola, southern Zaire, and Zambia. The

Flour worm: larva of various insects which breed in stores of meal or flour, especially the Mediterranean moth.

A Crimson Seedcracker.

A pair of Melba Finches, members of the genus *Pytilia*.

A Red-breasted Bluebill. This species can become quite quarrelsome during the breeding season.

"*. . .[The Bar-breasted Firefinch] is one of the most quarrelsome estrildid finches and should not under any circumstances be kept together with related species.*"

cock's plumage: brow, sides of the head rose-red; upper head and neck gray-brown; back somewhat purer brown; upper tail coverts brown (not red as with all other Firefinches); throat and breast rose-red, with numerous white darkly edged dots up to the feather root on the breast; back, breast and underbody gray-brown to gray, depending on the race; eye gray to brown; beak red, at the base lighter, with gray roof and blackish midsection of the lower beak; feet dark brown to gray. The hen is duller rose-red and the red on the sides of the head is less spread out.

The 10 cm long Bar-breasted Firefinch, *Lagonosticta rufopicta*, also known as the Bar-breasted Finch, is distributed from west Africa to the Upper Nile; it is similar to the Brown-rumped Firefinch, but with more red on the underside and with red upper tail coverts. Its breeding has also succeeded repeatedly. It is one of the most quarrelsome estrildid finches and should not under any circumstances be kept together with related species.

The Actual Red-billed Firefinch, *Lagonosticta senegala*, is one of the regularly and numerously imported, most well-known estrildid finches. Also called Small Red-billed Firefinch or Senegal Red-billed Firefinch, it is distributed from Senegal and Sudan throughout the largest part of Africa up to northern Namibia, to the Orange Free State and north Natal. It can also be found partly in the Cape area. It consists of nine races, of which the Estrildid Red-billed Firefinch, *Lagonosticta senegala ruberrima*, from east-central Africa is the easiest to identify by the dark red coloring of the cock; its hen has sides of the head with a touch of red; sometimes its throat and breast also have a touch of red; the hens of the remaining races are different shades of gray-brown with a white dotted breast and a red spot over the eye. Adult birds of both sexes always have a reddish beak, as is the case with the closely related Bar-breasted Firefinches. The cock can be distinguished from the common Bar-

A trio of Red-headed Finches. This species is said to be ideal for the aviary; it is, however, rarely available on the market.

breasted Firefinch by another shade of red coloring, rounder white breast dots, and by its song.

Red-billed Firefinches can live, once they have been acclimatized, up to ten years or longer in the cage or birdroom; most of these birds, however, die much sooner. Breeding them is relatively easy. In the wild, the Red-billed Firefinch is parasitized by the Red-footed Atlas Finch species, *Hypochera chalybeata*. For food the Red-billed Firefinch needs Senegal millet, spray millet, sprouted seeds, green food, etc., and some animal food; it does not, however, require as much animal food as other Red-billed Firefinch species. In its natural habitat, it often lives in the vicinity of human dwellings, builds its nests on and in buildings, and is also friendlier in captivity than many other estrildid finches.

The Rare Red-billed Firefinch or Black-bellied Firefinch, *Lagonosticta rara*, inhabits the savannah areas of eastern Sierra Leone and Nigeria to west Kenya. The male of this 11 cm long estrildid finch, which is rare on the market, has a burgundy-red plumage coloring with a black

Peter's Twinspot is difficult to find, but it is a hardy bird that breeds well in captivity.

"Red-billed Firefinches can live, once they have been acclimatized, up to ten years or longer in the cage or birdroom . . ."

Vane: the web or flat, expanded portion of a feather.

midsection of the underside; the lower tail coverts are also black. The hen is brown-gray with red upper tail coverts, red spot in front of the eye and more or less reddish faded plumage, depending on the race. Beak blackish, base of the beak reddish. This beak coloring and the black underbody midsection of the cock distinguish this Red-billed Firefinch species from the two following species. As they do, it requires much animal food and must be carefully acclimatized.

The Dark Firefinch, *Lagonosticta rubricata*, has the same size as the Black-bellied Firefinch and similar coloring. It also inhabits the tropical African savannahs to the south up to north Angola and through east Africa up to Transvaal, Natal and the southeastern and south Cape area. It has been imported frequently and has proven to be quite weak upon reaching its destination. It has a pretty song with trilling, warbling and flute-like phrases. The blue-gray beak (only the *Lagonosticta rubricata landanae* race from north Angola has a rose-red lower beak) and the black (instead of gray-brown) lower tail coverts of the cock distinguish it from common Red-billed Firefinches and both Bar-breasted Firefinches. Its beak coloring and the cock's limiting of the black underside coloring to under tail coverts and back stomach distinguish it from the Rare Red-billed Firefinch. The fact that all adult Dark Firefinches, with the exception of the Upper Niger race, *Lagonosticta rubricata virata*, show a sudden narrowing at the tip of the inner vane of the outermost flight feather is another

Peter's Twinspot, an attractive and steadfast species, is recommended for finch keepers. It must, however, be properly acclimatized to its new surroundings.

Peter's Twinspot ranges from eastern Africa to southern Mozambique.

"The red in the Dark Firefinch's coloring is darker amd more lively than that of Jameson's Firefinch. . ."

distinguishing characteristic. The Dark Firefinch's back is olive-brown or shale-gray; Jameson's Firefinch has in contrast a reddish or yellowy-brown back. The red in the Dark Firefinch's coloring is darker and more lively than that of Jameson's Firefinch, a frequently imported race; the hens of both species can be distinguished from each other only by the first-mentioned characteristic (the hens of the *L.r. virata* race, which do not show any narrowing of the outermost large flight feather, look more or less like the cock and can be differentiated by that and by the grayer back from Jameson's

An adorable pair of Rosy Twinspots. This species is infrequently available for sale.

A Red-billed Firefinch.

Nominative race: the subspecies within a species in which the trinomial scientific name has the same specific and subspecific name (e.g. Lagonostica larvata larvata*), indicating that this was the first race of the species to be identified.*

Firefinch hen). Breeding Dark Firefinches has succeeded repeatedly.

Jameson's Firefinch, *Lagonosticta rhodopareia*, is closely related to the Dark Firefinch and was for some time erroneously classified as being that bird. It is the substitute for the Dark Firefinch in drier regions and is distributed from Ethiopia to Angola, Transvaal and Zululand. While the cock of the rarely imported *Lagonosticta rhodopareia ansorgei* race from Angola is colored as lively red as the Dark Firefinch, although somewhat lighter, a more frequently imported race of this species, *Lagonosticta rhodopareia jamesoni*, distributed from Kenya to Transvaal and Zululand, is colored, in the male sex, paler rose-red or crimson red on the underside and on the sides of the head. The hen is colored like the hen of the Dark Firefinch—dirty yellow-red to salmon-reddish on the underside and, except for the shape of the outermost large flight feather (the ninth hand flight feather), is difficult to differentiate. Jameson's Firefinch has a nice song with little woodlark and wood dickybird-like phrases; that song is, however, not heard frequently. Jameson's Firefinch requires much animal food. When rearing young, to my knowledge, it likes above all fresh meadow ant pupae; breeding, however, has rarely succeeded. It needs light and warmth (20-25°C).

The Masked Firefinch, *Lagonosticta larvata*, in the past only very rarely imported, is distributed in several races from Senegal and Gambia to Ethiopia. Its nominative race differs greatly from the other races (dark brown-gray upperside; red nape collar; brow, sides of the head and throat black) and has its habitat in Ethiopia. The Wine-red-billed Firefinch, *Lagonosticta larvata vinacea*, from south Senegal to Guinea-Bissau, another race of that species, was for a time almost regularly available on the market and is currently imported now and then. Its length is about 11 cm. It differs considerably from the Red-billed Firefinches in plumage coloring. The cock's plumage: brow, sides of the head, throat black; upper head gray; back, wing coverts and underside bright wine-red; the breast white-dotted; under tail coverts black; tail feathers red; flight feathers dark brown; eyes brown; gray-blue lid rim; beak and feet lead-gray. The hen is pale brownish on the upperside, with a touch of weak wine-red; upper head gray; sides of the head and throat yellowy-gray.

The Wine-red-billed Firefinch has warbling alarm calls and, during the breeding season, unusual sobbing sounds, which are emitted with a closed beak. Its song resembles that of Jameson's Firefinch. This attractive firefinch is by nature especially charming, elegant, lively, and also friendly. It has to be carefully acclimatized, for which warmth and suitable food such as Senegal millet and spray millet, fresh ant pupae, egg food, and possibly boiled flour worms as well as all kinds of insects are necessary. Its breeding has succeeded repeatedly.

The Vinaceous Firefinch, *Lagonosticta larvata nigricollis*, from Ghana to southern Sudan, was

". . .[The Wine-red-billed Firefinch] is by nature especially charming, elegant, lively, and also friendly."

Peter's Twinspot. This species is also known as simply the Twinspot.

A Red-billed Firefinch. Once acclimatized, this species is very aggressive with similar species.

imported for the first time in 1965. Its body plumage is not wine-red, but rather with a touch of gray, crimson red.

The Red-cheeked Cordonbleu or Red-cheeked Finch, *Uraeginthus bengalus*, distributed from Senegal to Ethiopia and throughout east Africa to Tanzania, north Zambia and to southwestern Zaire in numerous races not differing much from each other, is one of the most frequently available finches on the market. Its total length is about 12 cm, with the tail measuring 5 cm of that length. The racial differences, shown in the distribution of brown and blue on the underside, are more easily detectable on the hen than on the cock. In the beginning, the Red-cheeked Cordonbleu is sensitive and should be carefully acclimatized.

"The Red-cheeked Cordonbleu . . . is one of the most frequently available finches on the market."

A Blue-headed Cordonbleu. This species is also known as the Blue-capped Cordonbleu.

After this first critical period, it is, however, quite modest and steadfast. Except in the breeding season, when it is incompatible with its own kind and other Red-cheeked Cordonbleu species, this attractive, lively finch proves to be a peaceful bird which gets along with its neighbors and which also becomes friendly and tame. Its flight is often butterfly-like, hovering and fluttering, especially before the landing. Its song consists of a short phrase.

It begins breeding in a larger area, ideally in an aviary, relatively easily, but leaves its eggs and chicks at the slightest disturbance. It does not begin breeding in a cage. Nevertheless it is bred frequently, and live rearing food is needed. The cone-shaped, roofed-over nest is built in the open or in a box. One of my pairs built its nest in a canary nesting box hanging in the thick branches of the birdroom. It covered over the nest completely, except for a small entry hole. In the next year, the same pair built a very artistic free-standing nest in birch branches. It had the shape of a reclining pear with an entry hole on the side. At a later time, this pair used a nest built by Society Finches in a budgerigar box.

A lovely Red-cheeked Cordonbleu, *Uraeginthus bengalus*.

"Except in the breeding season . . . [the Red-cheeked Cordonbleu] proves to be a peaceful bird which gets along with its neighbors and which also becomes friendly and tame."

A female Masked Firefinch.

The chicks are similar to the hen, meaning that they do not yet have the red spot on the ear, which appears on the cocks in the fifth to eighth week. Mixed breeds have been bred with numerous other finches such as the Common Waxbill, Melba Finch, Black-rumped Waxbill, the Gold-breasted Waxbill, and Dark Firefinch. Mixed breeds have also been produced with the closest relative, the Blue-breasted Cordonbleu or Blue Finch, *Uraeginthus angolenis*, which is distributed in several races from Angola, Zambia and east Tanzania to northern Namibia, Transvaal and Natal. It does not have a red spot on the ear and has a gray instead of

Brierbush: a barren, open area, usually having acidic soil, which contains shrubby plants having two seed leaves (family Ericaceae).

reddish beak. Otherwise, however, it is just like its relative in plumage coloring and nature.

Breeding it has also succeeded numerous times. The Blue-headed Cordonbleu or Blue-headed Finch, *Uraeginthus cyanocephala*, from east Africa is similar to the Blue-breasted Cordonbleu but has an entirely blue head and a red beak. It has been imported only rarely, but nevertheless has been bred often and successfully crossed with the above-mentioned species.

The Violet-eared Waxbill, *Granatina granatina*, is a brilliantly colored finch which is closely related to the Red-cheeked Cordonbleus. It is distributed in south Angola and southwest Zambia up to Namibia and to the Orange Free State as well as a small area in south Mozambique. Its length is about 13.5-14.5 cm, of which 6-7 cm is accounted for by the tail. The cock's plumage coloring: brow cobalt blue; crop black; sides of the head pink; upper tail coverts violet; upperside red-brown; chin, throat black; underside, upperside and lower tail coverts deep blue; eye and lid rim red; beak red; feet reddish gray. Hen totally duller, upperside gray-brown; underside yellowy-brown; throat and lower tail coverts whitish.

In the beginning, the Violet-eared Waxbill is very feeble and as an inhabitant of the warm, dry brierbush needs warmth and the greatest possible amount of light and sun during acclimatization and also later. For food it needs sprouted seeds, soft food, and tea, oatmeal gruel or rice gruel instead of drinking water. It is one of the best estrildid finch singers. Its song is trilling and twittering, similar to faraway lark songs or, according to W. Baars, to the song of the briergrass bird. The hen also sings, but its song is quieter and shorter. Unfortunately, this beautiful finch is only rarely imported. In general it is compatible, but not with its own kind or the closely related Purple Grenadier, and often not with Red-cheeked Cordonbleus.

Despite a number of difficulties, breeding has succeeded several times. W. Baars offered as food Senegal and silver millet, poppy, fresh ant pupae in the summer, and flour worms as well as fruit—apples, pears, and grapes were preferred. He also offered half-ripe grass seeds, mugwort, bird mites and groundsel. In the wild, the Violet-eared Waxbill is parasitized by the King's Whydah, *Tetraenura regia*.

The equally large Purple Grenadier, *Granatina ianthinogaster*, is found in east Africa from north Somalia to Tanzania and is an especially beautiful bird. Because of its blue underbody, it is also known as the Blue-bellied Purple Grenadier or the Purple Grenadier Finch. In nature, it resembles the Violet-eared Waxbill and, like it, the Purple Grenadier is incompatible with birds of its kind and closely related species. It has to be carefully

The Bar-breasted Firefinch is one of the most quarrelsome of all finch species; therefore, it should never be kept with close relatives.

Red-cheeked Cordonbleus.

The Gouldian Finch is probably the most sought-after finch due to its unique plumage pattern.

Parasitism: a close relationship between two or more organisms that can be beneficial to one or more of them, in birds it often involves taking over the nest of the host species.

acclimatized. It needs the same food as the Violet-eared Waxbill. Breeding it has succeeded several times. It is documented that the Purple Grenadier has been parasitized by the Straw Whydah, *Tetraenura fischeri*. Recently, the Purple Grenadier has shown itself to be a much more reliable and therefore much more successful breeding bird than the Violet-eared Waxbill.

The *Estrilda* genus contains the most generally known estrildid finches, which are often imported in large numbers. This genus also includes birds which can be especially recommended to the novice fancier because they do not require any special care and are compatible, aside from harmless quarrels.

The Lavender Waxbill, *Estrilda (Glaucestrilda) caerulescens*, distributed in west Africa from Senegal up to the Chad area, is one of the nicest and most attractive estrildid finches. Unfortunately, it is often in quite a poor condition after being imported, but is quickly acclimatized with proper care and is then a modest and steadfast bird, which needs, however, additional animal food. Its length is 10-11 cm. The Lavender Waxbill is an unusually lovable bird, always in motion, and its behavior reminds us of our titmouse birds. Like them, it climbs around and curiously inspects every corner. It soon becomes familiar with the keeper and becomes tame in a short time. Its sexes are difficult to distinguish by plumage coloring. The hen is said to have more white dots on the points. A certain differentiating feature, however, is the cock's flute-like call. Except during the breeding season, when the cocks fight each other violently, Lavender Waxbills are peaceful birds. Their behavior is unusual, when, especially in the evening, they sit next to each other, nod ardently and emit a whisper-like sound, followed by several two-syllable calls with a long drawn out end syllable "zi-tuh."

Breeding has been repeatedly

A Dark Firefinch. This species is known for its pretty trilling song, which is often described as being flute-like.

A Red-billed Firefinch. Once acclimatized, this species can live as long as ten years in captivity, quite a remarkable lifespan.

successful only in the birdroom. The nest is round, has a flying-in channel and a small round entry hole and is otherwise built very artistically. The clutch consists of four or five eggs. Additional animal food is needed as rearing food. Hybrids have been bred with the Red-billed Firefinch.

Another Lavender Waxbill is the rarely (but recently more frequently) imported Black-tailed Lavender Waxbill, *Estrilda (Glaucestrilda) perreini*, with a black tail instead of the red tail of the common Lavender Waxbill. It is found in several races from the Zaire, Angola, and southeastern Africa to Natal and the eastern Cape area. Breeding has seldom succeeded. The bird needs much warmth.

The Cinderella Waxbill, *Estrilda (Glaucestrilda) thomensis*, reached Europe (Switzerland) for the first time in a living condition in 1966. A Lavender Waxbill species with a black tail, red sides of the body and partly red beak, it inhabits only a few areas of west and southwest Angola.

The Black-cheeked Waxbill, *Estrilda (Brunhilda) erythronotos*, is an especially pretty and active species which is, unfortunately, rather weak and is not frequently

"The Black-cheeked Waxbill . . . is an especially pretty and active species which is, unfortunately, rather weak and is not frequently imported."

The Red-billed Firefinch, *Lagonostica senegala*, is one of the most well-known finch species, and it has nine races.

"Black-cheeked Waxbills are initially quite weak and must be most carefully acclimatized."

imported. Its length is 12-13 cm, of which the tail accounts for 5-6 cm. It is very similar in behavior to the Lavender Waxbills. The plumage coloring, the same for both sexes, is as follows: head and upperside gray; the upperside has fine dark faded wine-reddish diagonal lines, black facemask; stomach midsection, vent, lower tail coverts, thighs and remaining underside gray; sides crimson red; rump deep crimson red; outside flight feathers black-brown with blurred diagonal stripes; inner flight feathers light with more sharply visible stripes; tail black; eye red; beak and feet black. The cock's song is a soft, Lavender Waxbill-like "tuu-huh." Lives in the sun-drenched brierbush.

Black-cheeked Waxbills are initially quite weak and must be most carefully acclimatized. During acclimatization, warmth, dry seeds, soaked and sprouted seeds, animal food, ant pupae, and flour worms are necessary. Black-cheeked Waxbills need much light and sun. Up to now, breeding has seldom succeeded. The *E.(B.) erythronotos delamerei* race is imported most frequently. It is from east Africa. W. Hoesch imported for the first time in 1955 the *Estrilda (Brunhilda) erythronotos soligena* race from Namibia and southwest Angola. The

E.(B.) erythronotos erythronotos race from central South Africa has also been imported.

The Pink-bellied Black-cheeked Waxbill, *Estrilda (Brunhilda) charmosyna*, distributed from south Ethiopia to Tanzania, is very similar to the Black-cheeked Waxbill, but it is lighter and has no black on the stomach; it is only rarely imported and is often confused with the Black-cheeked Waxbill.

The Black-headed Waxbill, *Estrilda (Krimhilda) atricapilla*, also known as Little Black Head, is a finch which is available in the bird trade now and then. Its habitat is in Cameroon and Zaire to Kenya. Its length is 10-11 cm. Its basic plumage is gray; rump and upper tail coverts as well as the sides of the body partially covered by the wings, red; eye brown; beak black with a red spot on the root of the lower beak; feet black. At least initially, the Black-headed Waxbill is said to be somewhat fussy in its choice of food.

The Black-crowned Waxbill, *Estrilda (Krimhilda) nonnula*, which is closely related to the Black-headed Waxbill and has similar coloring, is distributed from Cameroon to west Kenya. It is more available in the bird trade. The red coloring of the sides of its body is less extensive and is almost completely covered by the

"At least initially, the Black-headed Waxbill is said to be somewhat fussy in its choice of food."

The Blue-breasted Cordonbleu, *Uraeginthus angolensis*, is the closest relative of the Red-cheeked Cordonbleu. This species is sometimes called the Blue Finch.

The Diamond Sparrow is an uncommon finch that commands a high price whenever it becomes available to fanciers.

The Java Sparrow, or Java Rice Bird, is known for its velvety plumage and is said to make a good companion for pet budgerigars.

wings. The *Estrilda (Krimhilda) nonnula nonnula* race (east Cameroon and Zaire to west Kenya) has white or whitish sides of the head and underside; the *E.(K.) nonnula eisentrauti* race (west Cameroon; smaller) and *E.(K.) nonnula elizae* race (Fernando Poo Island; larger) are light gray. The Black-crowned Waxbill is tough and steadfast, but often suffers from a poor condition of its plumage, which may be the result of insufficient sunlight or food lacking in vitamins. Its voice is very faint and unimpressive.

The Common Waxbill, *Estrilda (Estrilda) astrild*, is frequently offered by the bird trade because of its easy acclimatization, its peaceful nature even during the breeding season, its not too difficult breeding and its lively disposition. It is distributed in a large number of races (about 17), varying only slightly, in Africa from Sierra Leone and Ethiopia up to the Cape area and on St. Helena ("Little Helena Pheasants"), on the Cape Verde Islands, on Principe and Sao Tome, the Maskarens, Seychelles, in various parts of Brazil and even in one place in Portugal, where it has been acclimatized by human beings. Its length is about 10.5-12.5 cm. In plumage coloring it corresponds to the Black-rumped Waxbill; its tail, however, is mostly longer and not black, but rather brownish, and the upper and lower sides show a distinct diagonal stripe marking; the cock's lower tail coverts are black, the hen's are dark brown; and many races have a much more lively and extended red stomach midsection.

The song consists of a raw, short and warbling "zi-zi-schra" or a similar phrase. Regarding food, the Common Waxbill is not fussy, but does need additional animal food. It begins breeding relatively easily, especially in the aviary, but does not incubate reliably, at least not in the beginning. Nevertheless, breeding has succeeded in many instances.

The nest is built mostly free-standing; in my flight aviary, they built their artistic cone-shaped nest with a small roofed-over entry hole

A lovely Blue-headed Cordonbleu. This species is related to both the Red-cheeked and the Blue-breasted Cordonbleus.

"The Black-crowned Waxbill is tough and steadfast, but often suffers from a poor condition of its plumage, which may be the result of insufficient sunlight or food lacking in vitamins."

Jameson's Firefinch requires much animal food if it is to live a healthy life in captivity. Breeding this species has rarely succeeded.

The Bar-breasted Firefinch is a shy bird, especially when housed in a planted aviary.

Whydah: a mostly black and white African weaverbird, distinguished by long, drooping tail feathers in the male bird.

on the roof of a nesting box in the upper third of the aviary. Hybrids have been bred with a large number of other species, including the Red-cheeked Cordonbleu, the Orange-cheeked Waxbill, Black-rumped Waxbill, allegedly also with the Zebra Finch, the African Silverbill and the Red-browed Finch. The Common Waxbill is, in the wild, the most frequently parasitized bird by the Dominican Whydah, *Vidua macroura*.

The Black-rumped Waxbill, *Estrilda (Estrilda) troglodytes*, numbers among the most frequently kept and almost always available

A Masked Firefinch. This species is not often seen on the bird market.

A pair of Violet-eared Waxbills. This species needs to be kept in warm and well-lit quarters, as it is not one of the hardier finches.

"Breeding [Black-rumped Waxbills] has succeeded repeatedly, but is often thwarted by the extraordinary restlessness of these small finches; if they do not like the food, they will abandon even older nest chicks."

small estrildid finches; its length is only 9 to 10 cm. It is distributed from Senegal to Eritrea; a closely related species with a browner and only partially black beak, the Arabian Waxbill, *Estrilda (Estrilda) rufibarba*, lives in southwest Arabia. The Black-rumped Waxbill is probably the hardiest small estrildid finch, whose acclimatization is no problem. Generally speaking, both sexes have the same coloring; however, the cock's pink-red spot on the stomach is more distinct, especially during the breeding season. Both sexes also have the same song; it consists of melodic, whistling calls. Breeding has succeeded repeatedly, but is often thwarted by the extraordinary restlessness of these small finches; if they do not like their food, they will abandon even older nest chicks. The nest, built free-standing, is cone-shaped, artistic and often has an entry canal. It is situated mostly low over the earth floor or right on it. One of my pairs built a cone-shaped nest with a small entry hole without a canal in a canary nesting box. Both parents take turns incubating, in 11-12 days, the three or four egg clutch. Mixed breeds have been bred with Red-cheeked Cordonbleus, Common Waxbills, Orange-cheeked Waxbills, Black-headed Waxbills, Rosy-rumped and Red-browed Finches. In the wild, the Black-rumped Waxbill is also probably parasitized by the Dominican Whydah.

The 10 cm long Rosy-rumped Waxbill, *Estrilda (Estrilda) rhodopyga*, distributed in two to three races in east Africa to Eritrea, was not available for a long time, was never imported in large numbers, but has been for the last few years more available in the bird trade. The basic plumage of both sexes is fawn-brown with fine dark diagonal stripes; upper tail coverts red; large wing covert feathers and inner arm flight feathers red-edged on the outside; crop and stripe through the eye red; cheeks and throat white; eye brown; beak black; on the sides and on the root red; feet brown. The hen is distinguishable

A pair of Purple Grenadiers. These birds are often called Blue-bellied Purple Grenadiers or Purple Grenadier Finches.

A pair of Red-cheeked Cordonbleus. This species is quite peaceful and, once acclimatized, is capable of becoming friendly and tame towards its owner.

by the more gray-brown lower tail coverts. Rosy-rumped Waxbills are like the Black-rumped Waxbills in nature, mingling gladly with them and breeding easily with them. Breeding the Rosy-rumped Waxbill is easier than breeding Black-rumped Waxbills. It has succeeded repeatedly.

The Fawn-breasted Waxbill, *Estrilda (Estrilda) paludicola*, reached Europe for the first time in 1957, later more frequently. It is distributed in several significantly differing races from Ethiopia to Zambia and Angola. Its length: about 10 to 11 cm. The cock's plumage: upper head brown or more or less ash-gray, depending on the race; wings, back mostly fawn-brown with fine and blurred dark diagonal stripes; hind rump and upper tail coverts red; tail brown-black; outer feathers with light edges; sides of the head ash-gray to whitish or earth yellow; underside earth-yellowish to gray-white with a more or less rose-red tinge on the hind body, depending on the race; eye red or red-brown; beak red; feet brown. The *Estrilda (Estrilda) paludicola benguellensis* race from northern Angola, southern Zaire and north Zambia (upper head and sides of the head gray, back fawn-brown, underside earth-yellowish) has been imported. Mostly imported has been, however, one of the most modest and thankful estrildid finches, the starkly varying *E.(E.) paludicola ochrogaster* race from Ethiopia: upper head and back yellowish-gray-brown; throat lively yellow; remaining underside paler yellow; hind sides of the body, as with other races, light rose-red.

When a generic name is followed by another in parentheses, it means that some taxonomists use that name instead. Keep in mind that taxonomy is a constantly evolving science.

The Purple Grenadier has been successfully bred in captivity. Breeding, however, should not take place until it is absolutely certain that the birds have been carefully and completely acclimatized.

"Breeding [the Orange-cheeked Waxbill] is not very simple, because of the timidity of the bird."

Fawn-breasted Waxbills are always lively, tough and steadfast. In keeping with their habitat in high grass and reeds, vertically standing blades of reeds should be placed in the cage; the birds can use them to file down their rapidly growing claws. The Fawn-breasted Waxbill cock can be recognized by its extended rose-red coloring on the hind body. The first breeding succeeded in 1960. Food: Senegal millet and other seeds, also soft food.

The Orange-cheeked Waxbill, *Estrilda (Estrilda) melopoda*, has been regularly imported in large numbers. It is distributed from Senegal to north Angola and to eastern Zaire and even introduced to Puerto Rico. This estrildid finch is very lively, compatible and steadfast, but rather timid. Having a length of 9.5-10 cm, it is one of the smallest birds of that species. Both sexes have the same coloring. In addition to sharp warning calls, the Orange-cheeked Waxbill has a twittering or warbling song.

It should receive a variety of food, including seeds and animal food. Breeding is not very simple, because of the timidity of the bird. It should take place in a larger area. Breeding

A pair of Lavender Waxbills. This species is hardy in captivity but sometimes has a problem with feather plucking and melanism.

efforts have repeatedly succeeded. Nests are cone-shaped with an entry canal, which is often missing in captivity. Mixed breeds have been bred with Black-rumped Waxbills and Rosy-rumped Waxbills, allegedly also with other estrildid finch species.

"The Swee Waxbill . . . is rarely on the bird market. One of the smallest estrildid finches . . . it is distributed from Ethiopia throughout east Africa up to the eastern and southern Cape area and also in Angola."

The Swee Waxbill or Green Finch, *Estrilda (Neisna) melanotis*, is rarely available on the market. One of the smallest estrildid finches with a length of 9-10 cm, it is distributed from Ethiopia throughout east Africa up to the eastern and southern Cape area and also in Angola. The cock's plumage: upper head, neck gray; back olive-green; rump and upper tail coverts shining red; tail black; sides of the head, cheeks, throat black or light-gray, depending on the race; breast light-gray; underbody midsection light earth-yellow; on the sides more olive-green or gray; eye dark with red iris; upper beak black, lower coral-red; feet black. The hen's colors are duller.

The entire species *melanotis* was called Little Black Cheek in the past, despite its including several races which do not have black cheeks. Today only the two black-cheeked races are termed Swee Waxbill, namely the nominate form, *Estrilda (Neisna) melanotis melanotis*, to designate the bird which has its habitat in the region from Transvaal throughout Natal up to the southern Cape area, and also the lively colored *E.(N.) melanotis bocagei* race which

A Violet-eared Waxbill. Some experts feel that this species cannot tolerate drops in temperature or excessive dampness.

The Lavender Waxbill can become quite lovable and curious once it has been properly acclimatized to its new surroundings.

The Cinderella Waxbill is a member of the genus *Estrilda*.

"The Swee Waxbill has a pleasant nature, and is lively but quieter than other finches. It is also compatible."

Also known as Perrein's Waxbill, the Black-tailed Lavender Waxbill is rarely seen on the market.

lives in the region from western Angola to the most northern part of Namibia. This race has been imported and bred frequently in recent times. The hens of both these races do not have black coloring on the head. The Swee Waxbill has a pleasant nature, and is lively but quieter than other finches. It is also compatible. Its song is unimpressive. Its food is the same as that of the Orange-cheeked Waxbill.

The actual Green Finches do not have black cheeks. They are represented by the following species: the Zimbabwe Greenfinch, *Estrilda (Neisna) melanotis stuartirwini*, lighter and with a greener back, which lives in the mountain ranges and highlands of east Zimbabwe to south Tanzania; the East African Greenfinch, *E.(N.) melanotis kilimensis*, darker and with a more brownish back, which is at home in north Tanzania, Uganda and Kenya; and the greener Abyssinian Greenfinch, *E.(N.) melanotis quartinia*, which has its habitat in Ethiopia and is also named Little Earth-Yellow Breast. The underside of the first two birds is a deeper earth-yellow; the latter bird is a lighter, livelier, more lemon-yellow.

The two birds of the *Ortygospiza* species, the Quail Finch, *Ortygospiza atricollis*, and the attractive, rarely imported African Locust Finch, *Ortygospiza locustella*, have a way of life which is different from that of other estrildid finches.

The Quail Finch, *Ortygospiza atricollis*, is undoubtedly the best known of these two species. It is distributed in west Africa from Senegal to Nigeria and in east Africa from Sudan and Abyssinia to the eastern Cape area, also in Angola and in northern Namibia. With a length of only 9-10 cm, it is also one of the smallest estrildid finches. It is an avowed ground bird, running around like a quail (that is why it is so-named) between the clumps of grass, but not scratching like a chicken. The cock's plumage: brow, crop black; chin white; eye region differing, with either expanded white eyeglass marking or entirely

The Common or St. Helena Waxbill has a large distribution. It has even acclimatized to live in the wild in Portugal.

Maw: the crop, an enlarged pouch in the gullet in which food is ground, often with the aid of ingested sand or gravel.

without it, depending on the race; upperside gray-brown; short tail; head and neck sides gray-brown; throat and frontal cheek black; maw, upper breast and sides of the body with black-white diagonal bands; back breast reddish-brown; eye red-brown; upper side of the beak brownish-black; lower side red, entirely red during the breeding season; feet flesh-colored. Hen colored duller, without black on the head and throat.

The Quail Finch is sociable, quiet, compatible, friendly and tame. If it is kept in a cage, the cage must be roomy and have a soft cover lining the roof, since it thrusts itself upward like a quail and could injure its head if the cover is hard. Because of the Quail Finch's nervousness in the breeding season, breeding is

The sexes of the Black-cheeked Waxbill cannot be distinguished unless a male and female are side by side. The male has slightly brighter markings on its plumage.

Daphnia: members of the genus Daphnia, *small crustaceans, often called water fleas, that are commonly used as food in the aquarium hobby and in aviculture.*

difficult, but has succeeded repeatedly in the last few years. The nest is placed on the ground. Feeding is with seeds; during rearing plant lice, ant pupae, daphnia.

The species is made up of several races, of which the Partridge Finch, *Ortygospiza atricollis atricollis*, is one. It does not have any eyeglass marking but does have a white chin.

The races which are designated as actual Quail Finches all have a white eyeglass marking and are not very noticeably different from one another; the *Ortygospiza atricollis muelleri* race (hind breast and stomach midsection reddish-brown) from east-central Africa is imported most often; the *Ortygospiza atricollis fuscocrissa* race from Ethiopia is somewhat larger; the *Ortygospiza atricollis digressa* race from Zimbabwe and eastern South Africa is darker; the races *Ortygospiza atricollis bradfieldi* (northern Namibia to southwest Zambia and northwest Zimbabwe) and the paler *Ortygospiza atricollis pallida* have a red-brown hind breast and a white stomach midsection. The latter race is from the northern Kalahari Desert. The *Ortygospiza atricollis gabonenesis, O.a. dorsostriata* and *O.a. fuscata* races, living in Gabon and from north Angola to west Uganda and north Zambia, do not

The Black-rumped Waxbill is one of the most commonly imported African finches.

The Purple Grenadier has the same basic coloration as the Violet-eared Waxbill, but its ear patch is much smaller. The Grenadier also has a larger body.

The Rosy-rumped Waxbill, also known as the Crimson-rumped Waxbill, is similar in many respects to the Black-rumped Waxbill.

Plant lice: aphids or other small insects which have sucking mouthparts for ingesting plant juices.

have "eyeglasses" and have a black instead of a white chin. For a time, they were set apart from the others as a special species (Black-chin Quail Finch).

The 9-10 cm long (Red) Avadavat, *Amandava amandava*, distributed from India to south China and Timor, is regularly available in the bird trade. It is a modest, steadfast, compatible and lively small estrildid finch which can be highly recommended to the novicc fancier, since along with these other good qualities it has a pretty, trilling song which it emits diligently. The hen also sings, but more softly and usually only when a cock is not present. The (Red) Avadavat is fed with various kinds of millet, spray millet, sprouted seeds, and half-ripe grass seeds; when rearing, it eats hard-boiled egg, egg bread, ant pupae, plant lice. Fresh green food should also be offered. Once well acclimatized, the (Red) Avadavat breeds easily. Its nest is mostly free-standing in bushes, cone or bag-shaped. Clutch size is from four to six eggs; incubation time is 11-12 days. Often there are several incubations in succession. Keep in mind that the cock has two sets of plumage: a resting plumage, which

The Blue-breasted Cordonbleu is known simultaneously as the Blue-breasted Waxbill and the Cordonbleu.

The popular Zebra Finch is without a doubt one of the easiest finches to keep and breed in captivity.

A Yellow-headed Gouldian Finch.

A bevy of Gold-breasted Waxbills. It is often said that no two males of this species look alike.

is similar to the hen's plumage, and a breeding plumage, which is completely developed for the first time at two years of age. This is why we find (Red) Avadavat cocks at the pet shop with all kinds of plumage, from the plain resting plumage gray-brown on the upperside, whitish earth-yellow on the underside, through the various transition stages to the red breeding plumage. The specimens offered for sale which are called "deep (Red) Avadavats" are not a special (Red) Avadavat species, but rather freshly imported cocks which have not yet molted in captivity; in captivity, the birds usually take on only a copper-red breeding plumage, perhaps because certain foods are missing from their diet. The "Green Avadavats" appearing on the bird market are either Olive-green Finches, not Avadavats at all, or normal Avadavats which have been artificially colored green, which I have seen in a number of zoo shops. As one bird dealer told me, they come in from the exporting countries already in an artificially colored condition, for example pink or yellow, so that they can command higher prices as "rarities." Of course, it is the duty of the dealer to specifically call the artificial dyeing of these birds to the attention of the buyer, otherwise, he is guilty of fraud; the entire dyed-on glory disappears when the next molting takes place and the bird reveals itself to be a "normal" Avadavat, often a hen or only under the best of circumstances an attractive red Avadavat cock. Fortunately, artificial aniline dyeing of Avadavats and other small estrildid finches has almost stopped. In any case, the (Red) Avadavat tends to have color variations; many specimens in the cage become totally or partially black, probably because of the scarcity of sunlight; others get single white feathers.

The (Red) Avadavat is made up of

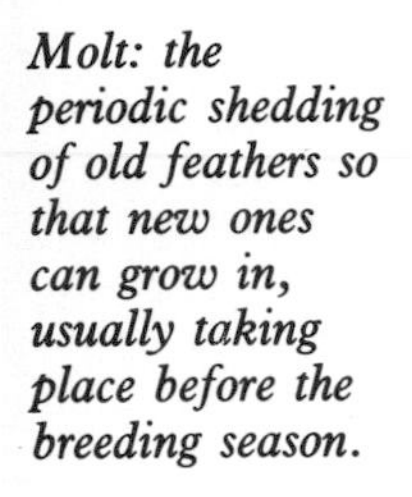

Molt: the periodic shedding of old feathers so that new ones can grow in, usually taking place before the breeding season.

A pair of Orange-cheeked Waxbills engaged in a preening session.

A pair of Black-crowned Waxbills.

". . .[The Gold-breasted Waxbill] is one of the estrildid finches most worthy of recommendation because it is, aside from its attractive plumage coloration, also very steadfast, compatible and easy to breed, even in a cage."

different races. The black-stomached Indian Avadavat, *Amandava amandava amandava*, lives in Near India to Assam; the also black-stomached Indonesian Avadavat, *Amandava amandava punicea*, called the Chinese Avadavat in the bird trade, lives on Java, Bali, in Cambodia, south Thailand, in southern Vietnam and on the Hainan Island (south China); whereas the Swee Avadavat, *Amandava amandava flavidiventris*, a yellow-stomached race, lives in Burma and on the Lesser Sunda Islands to Timor.

The Gold-breasted Waxbill, *Sporaeginthus subflavus*, is very closely related to the (Red) Avadavat. It has its habitat in Africa from Senegal and Ethiopia to Angola, Transvaal, Basutoland and Natal and also in southwest Arabia. It is mostly imported in the *Sporaeginthus subflavus subflavus* race from Senegal, which is replaced in Guinea and Sierra Leone and from Nigeria to Ethiopia by the *S. subflavus miniatus* race having an orange-red underside. The hen is duller and does not have the cock's eyebrow stripe.

The species is represented in east and southeast Africa to Lesotho and Natal by the *Sporaeginthus subflavus clarkei* race, having a purer yellow underside, while the still purer yellow undersided *S. subflavus niethammeri* race is found in Zambia and to south and central Angola. The Gold-breasted Waxbill is often offered in the bird trade. Its length is only 9-10 cm. It is one of the estrildid finches most worthy of recommendation because it is, aside from its attractive plumage coloring, also very steadfast, compatible and easy to breed, even in a cage. Its song consists of a sparrow-like "schilp" or "zilp" which is emitted without stopping, especially in the early morning, so that it can actually become annoying. Its song, with its "zilp-zalp, zilp-zilp-zilp-zalp" phrase, sounds like the song of the Zilpzalp (*Phylloscopus collybita*).

It is nourished with small millet varieties, including spray millet;

A Fawn-breasted Waxbill. This species seldom breeds well in captivity.

animal food is necessary, especially to rear the young; green food is also important. Mixed breeds have been bred with the (Red) Avadavat, allegedly also with the Red-billed Firefinch, the Red-cheeked Cordonbleu, the Common Waxbill, and the Black-rumped Waxbill.

The Olive-green Avadavat, *Stictospiza formosa*, belongs to a closely related species. It is from south-central India and is known in the bird trade also as the "Green Avadavat." The Olive-green Avadavat is a quiet and compatible bird, which spends much time on the ground or floor. It is not at all delicate and a cage age of eight to ten years is not unusual. The cock is olive-green on the upperside; upper tail coverts shining olive-yellow; head and sides of the neck pale yellow; sides of the body dark olive-green and white thin-striped; hand coverts and flight feathers black-brown and olive-green edged; tail black; beak red; feet reddish-gray. The hen is duller colored. The Olive-green Avadavat's length is about 10 cm. In its homeland, it builds its nest on reed and grass stalks. The nest is cone-shaped, rather large, and has a short pipe in front of the entry hole. Breeding is not so easy, but has succeeded frequently.

A Common Waxbill.

Green food: sprouted seeds or various fruits and vegetables which make wonderful supplements to the diet of estrildid finches, a necessity for some species.

The Red-browed Finch, *Aegintha temporalis*, consisting of three races, is from Australia—east Australia from Cape York to Victoria (it was introduced by human beings to a small area of Western Australia in 1960 or 1961, and has also been on Tahiti for a long time after having been introduced there by humans). Its length is 12 cm. The plumage of both sexes: upper head gray; back and wings gray-olive-green; rump and upper tail coverts shining red; tail black-brown; sides of the head and throat light gray; eyebrow stripe shining red; stomach midsection pale yellowish-gray, underside otherwise light bluish-gray; eye red; beak red with black roof; feet yellowy-horn colored. In past times, the Red-browed Finch was not imported frequently; since the export stop

A mutation of the Swee Waxbill, this species is called the Yellow-bellied Waxbill, *Estrilda melanotis bocagei*.

A Black-rumped Waxbill.

". . .[The Diamond Finch] is quiet and compatible, except during the breeding season when it often shows itself as a bad troublemaker."

ordered by Australia several years ago, this and other Australian birds are unfortunately no longer available at all in the bird trade. It is a quiet and peaceful bird which has been successfully bred repeatedly. It is reputed to be very feeble and does not reach old age very often.

The Diamond Finch, *Stagonopleura guttata*, has its home in eastern Australia from Victoria to south Queensland. It is 12 cm long and has coloring rich in contrasts (black-white-red), with brown coloring on the back and wings. It is quiet and compatible, except during the breeding season, when it often shows itself as a bad troublemaker. Its enticing call is flute-like; its song consists of deep bass sounds. During courtship, the head is pointed downward, so that the beak almost touches the breast. At the same time, it lets its song be heard, while the hen answers with high, flute-like sounds which resemble the enticing call. Breeding succeeds only in aviaries and birdrooms; there, however, mostly reliably, since these birds have been selectively bred in captivity only since the Australian export stop in 1960, producing generation after generation of birds. The unreliable wild birds are not available for breeding anymore. The Diamond Finches are not sensitive

A male Gold-breasted Waxbill.

to disturbances at the nest. It is difficult to bring together a real pair, since it is hard to distinguish one sex from the other. The hens are somewhat smaller and have weaker black breast band and eye stripes. The nest, which has a huge size, is built either free-standing or in a box, is thick-walled, and often has an entry pipe. The clutch consists of four to six eggs, mostly five, and is incubated in about 14 days. After changing color, they have to be removed from the old birds, because they are aggressively pursued by the latter. Diamond Finches drink like doves—noisily. Nourish with different millet varieties, grass seeds, and sprouted green food, egg food for rearing, and ant pupae.

A magnificent bird, the Painted Finch, *Emblema picta*, inhabits the dry areas of northwest and central Australia. Its length is about 10.5 cm. Its long, tapered and sharp beak, about 11 mm long, is conspicuous. The hen's plumage shows less red on the head and on the breast, and underside as well as sides of the body are not so black, but rather more brownish. Once well acclimatized, the Painted Finch is one of the hardiest Australian birds. It begins breeding easily, but often does not incubate reliably, so that not many incubations are successfully completed. The Painted Finch is nourished with small-grain millet, spray millet, egg food, small flour worms, ant pupae, green food, and especially bird mites. Song is warbling, enticing call chirping. They are rarely available because of the Australian export stop, but birds bred in the Federal Republic of Germany and Japan are occasionally offered for sale.

Australian export stop: a restriction that was placed on the capture and sale of all native Australian birds for the sake of preservation of species.

A pair of Gold-breasted Waxbills.

A pair of (Red) Avadavats, often called Strawberry Finches. The female bird is the one with the drab coloration.

Northern Australia and southern New Guinea are the habitat of the Crimson Finch, *Neochmia phaeton*, which consists of three races and is 12.5 cm long. The cock's plumage: brow red; crown darker or lighter gray-brown, depending on the race, with a touch of purple-reddish; nape reddish ash-gray; back and wings brown, with a touch of red; upper tail coverts shining red; middle tail

feathers red, outer tail brown; crop, sides of the head, throat, breast and sides of the body shining red; a few small white spots on the sides of the breast; black stomach midsection (*Neochmia phaeton phaeton* and *Neochmia phaeton iredalei* races), or white stomach midsection (*Neochmia phaeton albiventer* and *Neochmia phaeton evangelinae* races); eye light brown; beak red; base of the lower beak white; feet yellowish. The hen: upper head, back and wings ash-gray with a touch of reddish; breast and sides of the body gray. Especially during the breeding season, the Crimson Finch is very aggressive and can become a danger to fellow birds, so do not keep it in a community. Its song consists of humming and squeaking, followed by a short flute-like call. For food, the Crimson Finch needs additional amounts of seed such as millet and canary seed; it also needs plenty of animal food. The Crimson Finch needs plenty of warmth, especially during the breeding season. Breeding has succeeded extensively. Mixed breeds with Diamond Finches, Red-browed Finches, Star Finches and Long-tailed Grassfinches have been produced.

The Star Finch, *Bathilda ruficauda*, lives in northern Australia to south Queensland. Its length is about 11 cm. The hen is duller colored, has much less red. The song consists of soft humming and chirping and is sung with the bird's tail erect. River banks with vegetation are the habitat of the Star Finches. They like to dwell on river banks in rushes, reeds, or thick grass. In keeping with that, provide for them a few vertical perching materials such as rushes, or not too sturdy blades of reed or not too smooth branches, which they will gladly use not only in daytime but also for sleeping.

Breeding succeeds repeatedly; all available specimens today have been reared in captivity. The nest is built free-standing or in a nesting box. It is round, oval, also cone-shaped and sturdily constructed. In the case of undependable pairs, you can let

A pair of Orange-cheeked Waxbills. This species has been hybridized with several closely related finches.

"Especially during the breeding season, the Crimson Finch is very aggressive and can become a danger to fellow birds, so do not keep it in a community."

The Quail Finch, an interesting and attractive bird, is one of the smallest estrildid finches.

This male (Red) Avadavat may look like it is preparing for flight, but it is actually in the middle of a courtship display.

"The Cherry Finch is not weak, acclimatizes itself easily, is modest and in general compatible with its own kind and other species."

Zebra Finches rear young Star Finches. Mixed breeds have been bred with those birds as well as with the Crimson Finch, Parson Finch and Long-tailed Grassfinch. The Star Finch is nourished with millet varieties, canary seed, grass seeds, green food; for rearing, offer spray millet, soaked seed, soft food, ant pupae, and egg food.

The Cherry Finch, *Aidemosyne modesta*, is from eastern Australia in the area from central Queensland to southern New South Wales. Since the Second World War, it has been available in the bird trade frequently. Also known as the Cherry Astrild, it has a length of about 11 cm. The cock's plumage: brow and front crown dark crimson red; crop black; upper head dark brown; upperside brown; white diagonal striping on the rump; chin, upper part of the throat black; side of the head white with partially brown diagonal striping; underside white and also with diagonal striping, except for the stomach midsection and the lower tail coverts; eye dark brown; beak black; feet flesh-colored. The hen does not have the black chin and throat spot.

The Cherry Finch is not weak, acclimatizes itself easily, is modest

A pair of (Red) Avadavats. These birds can be quarrelsome during the breeding period.

A pair of Common Waxbills. Males have bolder markings than females; this fact is especially noticeable in the eyebrow patches.

Artist's rendering of a pair of Olive-green Avadavats, *Amandava formosa*.

and in general compatible with its own kind and other species. The song consists of several hardly audible sounds followed by a few flute-like calls. Especially in aviaries, breeding is not difficult. The cone-shaped nest is built free-standing as well as in nesting boxes. Clutch has three to five eggs; length of incubation about 12 days. As with most other estrildid finches, the Cherry Finch needs (in addition to seeds such as millet and canary seed) sprouted spray millet, egg food, ant pupae, and flour worms. Hybrids have been bred with the Zebra Finch, Long-tailed and Masked Grassfinch, Bicheno Finch and Indian Silverbill.

The Bicheno Finch, *Stizoptera bichenovii*, lives in northern and eastern Australia. It is not brightly colored but is a very attractively marked, 10 cm long estrildid finch. The hen has a thinner black band under the throat and breast. The Bicheno Finch is made up of two races, of which the White-rumped Bicheno Finch, *Stizoptera bichenovii bichenovii*, inhabits eastern and northeastern Australia, while the Black-rumped Bicheno Finch, *Stizoptera bichenovii annulosa*, also known as Lattice-winged Finch, lives in northwestern Australia. The Bicheno Finch is a likeable charge which becomes very friendly, is lively, very mobile, and is able to

"The Bicheno Finch is a likeable charge which becomes very friendly, is very lively, and is able to climb around like a titmouse."

Black-headed Munias will most likely require frequent claw clippings, as the toenails and scales on the feet grow quickly.

The Red-headed Gouldian Finch is the most commonly seen phase of this species in captivity.

climb around like a titmouse. This species is peaceful with other birds. It has a great need for warmth and should not be kept at a temperature of less than 20°C. It drinks noisily. Song: softly whispering, with occasional light calls. Frequently bred. Nest mostly free-standing. Clutch has four to seven eggs; length of incubation 11 days. Mixed breeds have been bred with the Zebra Finch, White-headed Munia, Long-tailed Grassfinch, Parson Finch, Cherry Finch, and Masked Grassfinch.

The Australian Zebra Finch, *Taeniopygia guttata*, is, except for the Society Finch, undoubtedly the most well-known estrildid finch. Its *Taeniopygia guttata castanotis* race inhabits the Australian continent except the southwest, the Cape York Peninsula and several coastal areas of the east, while its *Taeniopygia guttata guttata* race lives on the Lesser Sunda Islands. It is an attractive, brightly colored and friendly bird which finds its way in any situation, and is therefore very adaptable. It is a good and reliable breeding bird which can also be used for foster-parenting. The Australian Zebra Finch is especially suitable for the novice fancier. The hen does not have the orange-colored cheek spots, the zebra marking on throat and breast, or the drop marking on the sides of the body. As with the domestication of every animal, numerous Zebra Finch color mutations have occurred, especially in the last decades. There are color mutations in white, silver, spotted, masked or marbleset (white with "ghost marking"), cinnamon and custard, as well as penguin-colored. For my taste, the naturally-colored Zebra Finches are the most beautiful.

Breeding Zebra Finches is often quite productive, especially since they nest in every time of the year. Nest is round and artistically built, free-standing or in a half-open little nesting box. Clutch has four to six eggs; length of incubation about 12 days. The song sounds ventriloquist-like, the enticing call is a one-

A Diamond Finch, sometimes called the Diamond Firetail. This species is quiet and well behaved, except during the breeding season.

". . .[The Australian Zebra Finch] is an attractive, brightly colored and friendly bird which finds its way in any situation, and is therefore very adaptable."

A pair of Olive-green Avadavats. This species, related to the (Red) Avadavat, is rather quiet. It can have a long lifespan in captivity.

The Crimson Finch, *Neochmia phaeton*, is often classified as *Poephila phaeton*.

syllable squeaky cry sounding like a child's trumpet. Often this song is emitted for a long time and can become annoying. Zebra Finches are compatible; only during the breeding season do the cocks fight, hacking at each other and pulling out clusters of each other's feathers while emitting threatening calls. In the community cage or in the birdroom, they often drive other breeding pairs out of the nests. This is why they should be kept to themselves and bred as single pairs in their own cage. Mixed breeds have been bred with a large number of other species. Hybrid breeding with the closest relative, the Bicheno Finch, has succeeded especially easily, but the mixed breed offspring have proven up until now to be incapable of reproduction.

The Long-tailed Grassfinch, *Poephila acuticauda*, is one of the best breeding birds among the estrildid finches. It has been re-bred extensively and is now again available everywhere. There are two kinds of Long-tailed Grassfinches: the Yellow-beaked Long-tailed Grassfinch, *Poephila acuticauda acuticauda*, living in northwestern Australia; and the Red-beaked Long-tailed Grassfinch, *Poephila acuticauda hecki*, inhabiting the central areas of the Northern Territory. Interestingly enough, both geographical races differ from each other almost only by the beak coloring, which varies in a broad transition area from yellow to red, while in plumage coloring, they can be told apart only by the somewhat more intensive coloring of the *Poephila acuticauda hecki*. The length of the Long-tailed Grassfinch is about 16-18 cm, including the two hair-shaped, extended middle tail feathers. Distinguishing the sexes from one another is difficult, since the cock's allegedly somewhat larger black spot on the throat is not an absolutely reliable feature and the varying length of the tail points can also be misleading. The cock's singing and a somewhat more erect and therefore noticeable posture remain as distinguishing characteristics.

"The Long-tailed Grassfinch . . . is one of the best breeding birds among the estrildid finches."

The Painted Finch is said to have difficulty incubating its eggs once they are laid. Therefore, careful attention must be paid to the breeding diet and to surroundings throughout the entire breeding process.

The Star Finch, *Bathilda ruficauda*, is often classified under the genus *Neochmia*; it has been hybridized with several other breeds.

The basic plumage coloring of the Long-tailed Grassfinches is brown to wine-red and gray with black and white markings. They are especially recommended as charges not only because of their delicate plumage coloring and always smooth plumage, their peacefulness and modesty, but also because of their friendly nature, their liveliness, and, especially, their easy breedability in the cage and in the aviary. They are nourished with all kinds of millet and canary seeds and sprouts, plenty of green food, and, especially when rearing, animal food. The nest is built mostly in the little box; the clutch consists of four to six eggs, which are usually incubated for 14 days. The chicks fly out in about three weeks, but must remain with the parents for at least four more weeks. Hybrids have been bred with a number of other species.

The Parson Finch (Parson Grassfinch), *Poephila cincta*, a further member of the *Poephila* species, is distributed from northeastern Australia up to the most northern part of New South Wales. There are three races of these birds: the *Poephila cincta nigrotecta* race living on Cape York; the similar Black-rumped Parson Finch, *Poephila cinta atropygialis*, from north Queensland (except the area of Cape York); and the White-rumped Parson Finch, *Poephila cincta cincta*, distributed from central Queensland up to the most northern part of New South Wales.

The Parson Finch's middle tail feathers are extended only in short tips, so that its total length is only 11 cm. In plumage coloring it closely resembles the Long-tailed Grassfinch species, but is pure brown without wine-red hues and has a black beak. Here determining gender is also difficult. Unfortunately, the Parson Finch is not very peaceful, making it appropriate to keep them only in individual pairs, insuring that they are not close relatives. They also breed in a cage and need a sleeping nest in the flight aviary, since they are quite sensitive to bad weather.

The Cherry Finch is a hardy species which is not difficult to acclimatize or breed, especially if it is kept in an aviary.

A beautiful Diamond Finch, *Stagonopleura guttata*. This species is often classified as *Emblema guttata*.

"Unfortunately, the Parson Finch is not very peaceful, making it appropriate to keep them only in individual pairs, insuring that they are not close relatives."

The Bicheno Finch is friendly and mobile, a wonderful bird to observe in an aviary setting.

"The Masked Grassfinch is the most peaceful grassfinch of the Poephila *species and possesses in general the pleasant traits of the Long-tailed Grassfinch."*

Food is the same as for the Long-tailed Grassfinch. Breeds mostly reliably and without difficulties. Clutch has four to six eggs; incubation time 12-13 days. Length of chicks' time in the nest is 20–25 days. Numerous hybrids have been bred with this finch. Those bred with the Long-tailed Grassfinch are fertile, due to the close affinity, and produce (according to Steinbacher/Wolters), in the reverse crossing with one or both parent species, racially pure-looking Parson Finches or Long-tailed Grassfinches in the second generation.

The Masked Grassfinch, *Poephila personata*, which is made up of two races, is distributed in Northern Australia. One of these races, the Actual Masked Grassfinch, *Poephila personata personata*, inhabits western and central parts of the Northern Territory. The other race, the White-ear Grassfinch, *Poephila personata leucotis*, lives in northeastern Australia. The length of these grassfinches is 12 cm. As was the case with the two previous species, determining the sexes of the Masked Grassfinches is extremely difficult. The cock's song is the only sure sign. The Masked Grassfinch is the most peaceful grassfinch of the *Poephila* species and possesses in general the pleasant traits of the Long-tailed Grassfinch. Conversely, there are differing opinions about it as a breeding bird. The fact is that it does not breed as simply and as productively as the Long-tailed Grassfinch, and it breeds only in spacious aviaries with numerous nesting places, whereby low bushes over the ground are preferred. Nevertheless, breeding has succeeded often, including mixed breeding with the Zebra Finch and the Long-tailed Grassfinch, and those with the latter bird have proven to be fertile. As rearing food, in addition to millet and canary seed, provide spray millet sprouts, a good soft food, some hard-boiled egg, flour worms, and plenty of green food.

The Gouldian Finch, *Chloebia gouldiae*, most likely the most

A pair of Yellow-beaked Long-tailed Grassfinches, *Poephila acuticauda acuticauda*. The sexes of this species are not easy to tell apart.

A pair of Bicheno Finches. This beautiful species is also known as the Owl Finch or the Double-bar Finch.

A pair of male Australian Zebra Finches, a normal and a fawn. Note the orange cheek spots, characteristic markings which help differentiate the sexes.

Polymorphous: multi-formed, meaning that animals of a given species can have several different appearances.

beautiful and most popular estrildid finch, has its habitat in the Northern Territory excepting the Cape York Peninsula. Its total length is about 14 cm. This finch is a polymorphous (i.e. multi-formed) species which has, based on the varying coloring of the head, a number of different coloring variations. These cannot be termed geographical races because they occur next to each other in a population of Gouldian Finches, which together inhabit a certain area and which also breed with one another. The most common variation in Australia is the Black-headed Gouldian Finch; the Red-headed Gouldian Finch is less frequent, in ratio about 1:3; and the Yellow-headed Gouldian Finch is a rarity (1:3000). Re-breeding in captivity has resulted, through selective popularity, in the reverse sequence, i.e. Red-headed, Black-headed, according to supply and demand. The sexes are easy to tell apart, as the hen has a duller coloring, the blue band on the back of the head is thinner or is completely missing, and yellow of the underbody is paler.

The Gouldian Finch is a quiet bird, friendly but does not become tame; it is mostly peaceful with other estrildid finches, even during the breeding season when, however, it does become quite lively. Once acclimatized, it is not a weakling, but does need a great deal of warmth and is very sensitive to raw, damp and cold weather. Food: millet, canary seed, spray millet, green food, soaked and sprouted seeds—poppy and lettuce seeds are also accepted. Soft food, egg, ant pupae, and flour worms are not favorite foods, but for better breeding

Above: **A Star Finch.**

success, the Gouldian Finches should be trained to accept them. They drink water noisily, like doves. As breeding birds they vary in suitability; some are reliable, others are total failures.

The parrot finches (*Erythrura* species) are almost as beautiful as the Gouldian Finch. They are distributed in an area from southern Tenasserim to Malakka and up to the Greater Sunda Islands and New Guinea and numerous islands of the Pacific Ocean. Parrot finches have a more or less thick-set figure, and have a thick beak, which has differing shapes, depending on the species. The shape and length of the tail are also different—some species have wedge-shaped tails, others have very short, broadly rounded-off tails, and some have tails with long drawn-out thin middle feathers. The total length of the bird depends on the length of the tail feathers; in the case of the short-tailed birds, it is about 10 cm, while it measures up to 15 cm in the case of the long-tailed species.

The Masked Grassfinch is the most peaceful of the grassfinches, but it does not breed as easily as some of its relatives.

A Parson Finch. This species is also known as the Black-throated Finch.

The parrot finch genus contains a number of birds which are rarely available in the bird trade and therefore command high prices. Little is known about their management and care, so that I would like to touch briefly on these species just to round out the picture. They are not suitable for the novice fancier.

Kleinschmidt's Parrot Finch, *Erythrura kleinschmidti*, from the Fiji Islands, is short-tailed, about 10 cm long and is an insect-eater, despite its thick beak. Like all parrot finches, it has a green basic plumage, a black mask, dark blue crown, red rump. Peale's Parrot Finch, *Erythrura pealii*, also from the Fiji Islands, has about the same size, and it has been available at different times in recent years. It has a crimson red upper head and sides of the head, black throat, blue front neck and a red rump. Living on the New Hebrides, the Royal Parrot Finch, *Erythrura regia*, resembles Peale's; the cock of the *Erythrura regia regia* race has, however, an

A pair of white Zebra Finches. The shorter bird is a chestnut-flanked white.

Genus: taxonomical rank, between family and species, based on evolutionary similarities between related species; a unique species with isolated characteristics can be given its own genus within its particular family.

A Red-beaked Long-tailed Grassfinch, *Poephila acuticauda hecki*. This species is related to the Parson Finch.

". . .[Young Red-headed Parrot Finches] do not have to be separated from the parents, since they are very peaceful among each other."

entirely blue back and also a blue underside. Imported for the first time in 1934, first breeding was successful in 1936. The nest was closed in a cage with a slanted entry pipe; rearing food included soft food, flour worms, fruit, and green food. In the wild, this species specializes in eating fig seeds and therefore has a rather fastidious taste when it comes to food; its diet needs to be supplemented with insects. Having equally fancy tastes in food is the Short-tailed Parrot Finch, *Erythrura cyaneovirens*, from Samoa. It closely resembles the Royal Parrot Finch.

In contrast to the fore-mentioned birds, the Red-headed Parrot Finch, *Erythrura psittacea*, is quite well-known. Its length is about 12 cm. Its brow, front crown, sides of the head and throat are red, as well as the hind rump, the upper tail coverts and the middle pointed tail feathers. As a whole, the hen is duller colored. This finch, which is available today as rather high-priced bred specimens in the bird trade, is one of the birds which can be highly recommended for the aviary, because it is extremely lively and mobile, peaceful, and its breeding is not too difficult. It needs, however, plenty of room. Telling the sexes apart is difficult. The cock can be recognized with certainty only by its long, drawn-out trilling enticing call, which is sung only briefly by the hen, which generally shows less red on the head.

The Red-headed Parrot Finch is nourished with a usual ready-mixed estrildid finch food as well as canary seed and some green food; fruit such as oranges, apples, and figs are also gladly accepted. For rearing: flour worms, sprouted seeds, ant pupae, egg, and egg bread. It likes to build its artistic nest in a nesting box. The clutch consists of four or five eggs, the incubation period is 13-14 days, and the young leave the nest at an age of about three weeks. After that, they are fed by the parents for another two weeks. They do not have to be separated from the parents, since they are very peaceful

Peale's Parrot Finch is sometimes available on the bird market. It, however, like most parrot finch species, is not very common.

A Black-headed Gouldian Finch.

A White-headed Munia. Note the striking bill color on this bird.

The Chestnut Munia is commonly kept in captivity. Members of its various subspecies are frequently available on the market.

Bicheno Finches are described as having delightfully pleasant personalities. They are noted for their congeniality.

". . .[The Blue-faced Parrot Finch] possesses all pleasant sides of the other species, is hearty and steadfast, modest and peaceful."

among each other. Mixed breeds have been bred with various other parrot finch species.

The Blue-faced Parrot Finch, *Erythrura trichroa*, is a bird worthy of recommendation. It lives in numerous races on Celebes, the Moluccas, New Guinea, in northeastern Australia, on the Bismarck archipelago, in Micronesia, on Guadalcanal, New Hebrides, etc. This pointed-tail parrot finch is 12-13 cm. Plumage color: basic plumage grass-green; brow and sides of the head blue; rump and upper tail coverts red. The hen is generally duller, with less blue on the brow. This parrot finch possesses all pleasant sides of the other species, is hearty and steadfast, modest and peaceful. It is, however, more highly spirited and should be kept in an area with plenty of space. Breeding is easy; it incubates very reliably. Provide the same food as the previous species. Clutch has four or five eggs, length of incubation 14-15 days; nest chicks stay in the nest 21-25 days. Mixed breeds have been bred with other parrot finches.

Recently, a very rare parrot finch came via H. Bregulla into the possession of Dr. Burkard and in the meantime into the hands of several German breeders, namely the Mindanao Parrot Finch, *Erythrura coloria*, which was first described in 1961 and which inhabits the mountain forest glades on Mount Katanglad on the Philippine island of Mindanao. It is mainly green-colored with a short reddish tail, red upper tail coverts, blue brow and blue sides of the head as well as a large, half-moon shaped red spot behind the blue sides of the head,

A Red-headed Gouldian Finch. The Gouldian Finch is one of the most popular finch species, due to its unusual coloring.

The Blue-faced Parrot Finch is not easy to find, but it is more readily available than most other parrot finches except the Red-headed Parrot Finch.

A Pin-tailed Parrot Finch. This species is very mobile and is recommended for keeping in an aviary.

which has resulted in it being named Red-eared Parrot Finch. Dr. Burkard has bred this parrot finch.

The Pin-tailed Parrot Finch, *Erythrura prasina*, has its habitat in upper India from Tenasserim and north Laos to Malaya, Sumatra, Java and Borneo. Due to the long tail points, its length is 14-15 cm. The hen does not have any blue parts of the plumage on the head, is gray to brownish-gray on the underside, and the middle tail feathers are not so strongly extended. The cock of the Yellow-stomached Parrot Finch is a not very rare color mutation with an orange-yellow instead of shining red underbody. When freshly imported, the Pin-tailed Parrot Finch is feeble, but once acclimatized, proves to be hardy and steadfast. It nourishes itself exclusively with seeds and does not require any animal food when rearing. Offer canary and millet seeds and sprouts, shelled oats, all kinds of half-ripe seeds, perhaps shelled rice, sprouted oats and wheat, plenty of green food, and fruit such as small pieces of apples and oranges.

Because of their great mobility, the Pin-tailed Parrot Finches should ideally be kept in a larger flight aviary with many plants to really bring out their beauty. Since these finches are generally peaceful with their own kind and with relatives, they can be kept together with other pairs. A successful breeding is not quite simple; it often takes years to succeed. Nevertheless, this species has been bred frequently. The

"Because of their great mobility, the Pin-tailed Parrot Finches should ideally be kept in a larger flight aviary with many plants to really bring out their beauty."

". . .the song of these not very sensitive [Green-tailed Parrot Finches] . . . is partially inaudible to the human ear. . . ."

relatively large nest is built free-standing or in a nesting box and has a small entry hole. Clutch has two to four eggs, length of incubation 20 days. Hybrids have been bred with the Red-headed and Blue-faced Parrot Finch as well as the African Silverbill.

The Green-faced Parrot Finch, *Erythrura viridifacies*, is similar to the Pin-tailed Parrot Finch and is from the northern part of Luzon Island (Philippines). It was first discovered in 1935 and was found again and described by H. Bregulla in 1966. It is grass-green, with a red tail with extended middle feathers, and with earth-yellowy lower tail feathers. The hen is duller colored and the middle feathers of the tail are shorter. A number of these rare birds were added in 1966 to the collection of Dr. Burkard, the well-known Swiss estrildid finch breeder.

The Green-tailed Parrot Finch, *Erythrura hyperythra*, also known as the Bamboo parrot finch, lives in various races in the mountains of Malaya, Java, Borneo, Celebes, the Lesser Sunda Islands and the Philippine islands of Luzon and Mindoro. It is green-colored on the upper side, black only on the brow and blue on the front crown, on the undersides and on the sides of the head ochre-brown. In 1931, the Berlin Zoo acquired a specimen of the Celebes race, *Erythrura hyperythra microhyncha*, and recently Dr. Burkard acquired some specimens of the Philippine race, *Erythrura hyperythra brunneiventris*. In the wild, the Green-tailed Parrot Finch prefers to stay in bamboo thickets. Dr. Burkard found that the song of these not very sensitive birds is partially inaudible to the human ear, which also applies to the phrase

A pair of fawn Java Sparrows.

A beautiful White Finch, a form of the Java Sparrow.

A male Blue-faced Parrot Finch.

"Out of the breeding season . . . [the Java Sparrow] is harmless and peaceful; it can turn into an evil nest robber during the breeding time and therefore should be kept together with birds of the same size as, for example, budgerigars only in roomy aviaries."

The Red-headed Parrot Finch is one of the more well-known parrot finch species. It is lively, peaceful, and a relatively easy breeder.

of the White-headed Munia. The birds kept by Dr. Burkard accepted almost solely canary seed, spray millet, and green food. In the wild, the main food is bamboo seeds.

Northwestern Australia eastwards to northwest Queensland is the habitat of the Pictorella Finch, *Heteromunia pectoralis*. Plumage: on the upperside brownish-silver-gray; undersides wine-reddish-gray; sides of the head, throat black; front breast white; the individual feathers with black band; eye dark brown; beak blue-gray; feet flesh-colored. Length about 12 cm. Hen less deep black on the head and throat; white thorax with thin black stripes. The Pictorella Finch has become almost extinct in home aviaries because it is a very difficult charge and is especially hard to begin breeding. It is nourished with millet, half-ripe grass seeds (for example, panicle grass), sprouted seeds, and green food; for rearing it receives plenty of flour worms, ant pupae, and egg or egg bread. Clutch has three or four eggs, length of incubation 14 days, length of nestlings 22 days.

The Java Sparrow or the Java Finch, *Padda oryzivora*, is a very well-known estrildid finch which inhabits Java and Bali but which has also been acclimatized to many areas of south Asia, the coastal areas of east Africa and to St. Helena. Its total length is about 14 cm. Both sexes have the same coloring; the only sure differentiating feature is the quite nice song of the cock, comparable to the ringing of little bells; trying to recognize the cock by its broader-arched upper beak takes some practice.

The Java Sparrow has been bred for centuries in China and Japan in a popular purely white form, the White Finch. It is a very pretty bird, carries its plumage smoothly, and is a decoration for the birdroom or cage. Out of the breeding season it is harmless and peaceful; it can turn into an evil nest robber during the breeding time and therefore should be kept together with birds of the same size as, for example, budgerigars only in roomy aviaries.

Regarding food, it does not have any special wishes. Millet (especially the large grain kinds), canary seed, and all kinds of green food are sufficient, even for rearing; it is, however, better to include animal food and sprouted seeds. In contrast to the easy breedability of the white cultivated finch, breeding the wild type is not at all easy, and it does not succeed as often as might be thought. The nest is artistic, often arched over, with a large entry hole. It is often built in larger nesting boxes. My Java Sparrows built their nests repeatedly in normal budgerigar boxes. Clutch has five or six eggs, length of incubation 13-15 days, length of nestlings four weeks. The chicks have a black beak; the White Finch chicks have pink beaks. The breeding of the White Finches produces mostly venison-colored or more or less gray piebald offspring, some with a touch of weak gray. Mixed breeds have been bred with the Society Finch, the Spice Finch, and the African Silverbill.

The Brown Java Finch, *Padda fuscata*, living on Timor and Saman (Lesser Sunda Islands) is, with a length of 12 cm, smaller than the Java Sparrow. In 1939, the Berlin Zoo acquired one specimen. Besides being smaller, it differs from the Java Sparrow by its chocolate-brown instead of gray plumage coloring, by its lead-gray lid rim, blue-gray beak, and horn-colored feet.

The Chestnut Munia, *Lonchura malacca*, is almost always available in several races in the bird trade. It is distributed in Ceylon, in lower and upper India, in southern China, on Sumatra, Java, Borneo, Celebes, the Philippines, and on Formosa.

The Three-colored Munia, *Lonchura malacca malacca*, inhabiting Ceylon and southern India, is one of the most well-known birds of these races. Its length is about 11-12 cm. It is quite attractive, peaceful, modest, and is nourished with millet, canary seed and sprouts, and green food. For rearing, only during the first days does it need egg food and/or rearing food with insects.

A Three-colored Munia. This species is rather well known and is often available on the market.

". . .[The Three-colored Munia] is quite attractive, peaceful, modest, and is nourished with millet, canary seed and sprouts, and green food."

The Pin-tailed Parrot Finch has been hybridized with several species of parrot finch.

The Java Sparrow is generally a peaceful bird, but it can be rather nasty during the breeding season.

A female Mindanao Parrot Finch. This species takes its name from the Philippine island it calls home.

The chestnut-brown and black-colored Black-headed Munia, *Lonchura malacca atricapilla*, is the most frequently imported and least expensive munia. It has its habitat in northeastern lower India to west Burma. Other races of this bird include the *Lonchura malacca deignani* from Thailand, with less black on the stomach, and the light brown *L.m. sinensis* from Malaya and parts of Sumatra, with still less black on the stomach, which is also imported frequently. Both sexes of this bird have the same coloring. The cock's ardent song can be more easily seen than heard because its beginning scale of notes is too high for human ears to pick up. Food is the same as that of the Three-colored Munia. Breeding has succeeded repeatedly, but is not simple, which

(Red) Avadavats are also known as Tiger Finches.

"The [Black-headed Munia] cock's ardent song can be more easily seen than heard because its beginning scale of notes is too high for human ears to pick up."

A lovely Java Sparrow.

A male Pictorella Finch. This species is very difficult to keep and is even harder to breed.

applies to all munias. Mixed breeds have been bred with a number of other estrildid finches, especially with Society Finches. Several other races very similar to the Black-headed Munia live in other parts of south and southeast Asia.

The Chestnut Munia (Black-throated Munia), *Lonchura malacca ferruginosa*, from Java and Bali, is available only rarely to the fancier. Its basic plumage is also chestnut-brown, but is duller; the head is whitish; throat and front breast black. This munia is also peaceful, modest, and steadfast. It is rarely bred. Like the other munias, it needs a quite roomy aviary with plenty of plants to breed successfully. The same food as for the Three-colored Munia is given. The song consists of a quiet humming, several notes accompanied by clapping of the beak, and, finally, quiet calls.

The White-headed Munia, *Lonchura maja*, lives in an area from Malaya, Sumatra, Java and Bali. It is just as large as the Chestnut Munia and is similar to it in plumage coloring, but has less black on the stomach. The hens can be recognized by the not pure white coloring with a touch of gray on the back head. This munia is also peaceful, steadfast, and modest. Its voice is distinctive, with the song beginning completely without a note and ending with a rather loud melodic call which is common to

". . .[The White-headed Munia] is . . . peaceful, steadfast, and modest. Its voice is distinctive, with the song beginning completely without a note and ending with a rather loud melodic call which is common to most munias."

A quartet of munias—two Black-headed Munias (*Lonchura malacca atricapilla*) and two White-headed Munias (*Lonchura maja*).

"[The Yellow-rumped Finch] is rarely available; it must be well acclimatized. It is quite peaceful."

most munias. When the bird begins to sing, you can see it moving its beak and ruffling its throat feathers, but you cannot hear it.

Breeding has succeeded repeatedly, clutch three to five eggs, length of incubation twelve days, length of nestlings 24-25 days. Mixed breeds have been bred with Society Finches, Chestnut-breasted Finches, Black-headed Munias, White-backed Munias and Parson Finches.

The toenails of all munias grow very thick, so that they have to be clipped from time to time to avoid accidents caused by the birds clinging to things. To an extent, this situation can be improved by putting bundles of reed, which are used by the munias for sitting and nesting, in the aviary.

The Yellow-rumped Finch, *Lonchura flaviprymna*, inhabits the western and central parts of the Northern Territory. Length about 11 cm. Both sexes have the same coloring. This bird is rarely available; it must be well acclimatized. It is quite peaceful. Breeding by experienced fanciers has succeeded repeatedly.

The Chestnut-breasted Finch, *Lonchura castaneothorax*, inhabits northern and eastern Australia and has been acclimatized in New Caledonia. The plumage: upper head, nape, hind neck gray-brown; back cinnamon-brown; rump strap-yellow to yellowy-brown; sides of the head and throat black; crop and front breast light chestnut-brown, with a black diagonal stripe dividing

The Long-tailed Grassfinch is also known as the Shafttail.

A pair of Zebra Finches. Zebra Finches have much to offer both the beginner and expert alike.

Cut-throat, or Ribbon, Finches must be kept in spacious quarters, as overcrowding often causes plucking.

A fawn Zebra Finch with a yellow beak. Zebra Finches have been hybridized with several other species, but the natural coloration is the most attractive.

it from the white stomach; lower tail coverts black; eye brown; beak and feet lead-gray. Length about 11 cm. Telling sexes apart is difficult; cock can be recognized by its song.

This bird is again regularly available because of new breeding. This compatible Finch is nourished in the same way as the previous birds. Breeding is not difficult. Clutch three to seven eggs, length of incubation 12-14 days, length of nestlings about three weeks. Hybrids have been bred with the Zebra Finch, Masked Greenfinch, African Silverbill, White-headed Munia, Society Finch, and the Yellow-rumped Finch.

The Spice Finch, *Lonchura punctulata*, is one of the most common birds available on the market. It is distributed in numerous races in lower and upper India, on the Sunda Islands, except Borneo, on Formosa, and in the most southern area of China. Its length is 12 cm. Its plumage is brown with different hues, depending on the race, with a scale-marked underside. The beak is lead-gray with a blackish roof, feet blue-gray. Both sexes have the same coloring. The Spice Finch is easy to acclimatize, friendly, steadfast, modest, and peaceful and can be especially recommended to the novice fancier. Only its breeding is difficult and has often succeeded only after a successful incubation with other species such as, for example, Society Finches. Clutch three to five eggs, length of incubation 13 days. Mixed breeds with the African Silverbill, Society Finch, Java Sparrow, Indian Silverbill, Bib Finch, Bronze Mannikin, Black-headed Munia, and the White-backed Munia.

"...[The Spice Finch's] breeding is difficult and has often only succeeded after a successful incubation with other species such as, for example, Society Finches."

A Black-headed Munia, *Lonchura malacca atricapilla*. Note the striking contrast between the jet black head and the shining gray beak.

This subspecies of the Chestnut Munia, *Lonchura malacca ferruginosa*, is also known as the Black-throated Munia.

The Bronze Mannikins are a many-race species of birds similar to the Munia. In the past, they were more frequently available on the bird market and deserve our interest because one Bronze Mannikin species is the basic race of the well-known Society Finch bred originally in Japan. Aside from that, Bronze Mannikins are charges worthy of recommendation, since they are quite lively, peaceful, modest, steadfast, and prove to be very willing to breed once they have been acclimatized. For breeding they require, however, larger areas, ideally a roomy flight aviary. They are nourished with millet and canary seed and sprouts, and plenty of green food, and ant pupae. Bronze Mannikins do not always accept flour worms.

Hill Bronze Mannikins, *Lonchura kelaarti*, live in southern India and Ceylon. In recent times, this species and especially its *L.k. jerdoni* race from southwest India have been occasionally imported. That race is brown on the uppersides, black on the sides of the head, throat and front breast, light wine-reddish-yellowy-brown on the underbody with some dark striping on the back stomach.

The White-bellied Bronze Mannikin, *Lonchura leucogastra*, living in Malaya, on Sumatra, Borneo and the Philippines, has a length of 12 cm. It has been rarely imported. Basic plumage brown-black; stomach midsection white; beak on the upper side blackish, on the underside gray-bluish; feet lead-gray. It very much resembles the White-backed Bronze Mannikin but has a dark rump and a shorter tail with yellow-edged feathers. It is often not recognized in the shipments. Little is known about its management, care, and breeding.

The Java Bronze Mannikin, *Lonchura leucogastroides*, is about the same size and has its habitat on the Sunda Islands from south Sumatra to Lombok. It has also been acclimatized in Singapore. It has a black front head, black throat and upper breast. It has not been

A pair of Yellow-rumped Finches. This species must be well acclimatized if it is to be kept successfully in captivity.

A pair of Swee Waxbills. Some finches will become quite friendly toward each other.

". . .Bronze Mannikins are charges worthy of recommendation, since they are quite lively, peaceful, modest, steadfast, and prove to be very willing to breed once they have been acclimatized."

The Masked Grassfinch is not as well known as but is quite similar to the Long-tailed Grassfinch.

". . .the oldest domesticated small bird [The Society Finch] is hardy, steadfast, modest, extremely willing to breed—all reasons why the novice estrildid finch fancier should begin with this bird."

imported since the Second World War.

The White-backed Bronze Mannikin, *Lonchura striata*, consists of numerous races and has a distribution area which extends from lower and upper India to north Sumatra, southern China and Formosa. The White-rumped Bronze Mannikin, *Lonchura striata striata*, lives in southern and central lower India; the Actual White-backed Bronze Mannikin, *Lonchura striata acuticauda*, lives in northern Near India; two additional races, the Rear-Indian White-backed Bronze Mannikin, *Lonchura striata subsquamicollis*, and the Chinese White-backed Bronze Mannikin, *Lonchura striata swinhoei*, have their habitat in Indonesia to Malaya and southern China, respectively. These two races are likely the progenitors of the Society Finch.

The Society Finch (four breeding races), bred for several centuries in China and later also in Japan, reached Europe about 100 years ago. This cultivated bird, the oldest

The Spice Finch is quite common in captivity and is often available on the market.

domesticated small bird, is hardy, steadfast, modest, extremely willing to breed—all reasons why the novice estrildid finch fancier should begin with this bird. The Society Finch is especially valued for its foster-parenting, where it can step in to incubate the eggs of other birds or rear the young of other birds if the estrildid finch parents should prove to be undependable or otherwise be incapacitated. Here it is especially advantageous that the Society Finch as a domesticated bird breeds the whole year 'round, with the exception of the molting time. A prerequisite, however, is that the finches have clutches or young in the nest at the same time as the other breeding birds. If compelled to use them as foster-parents, switch the entire clutch or all chicks, i.e. remove all of the Society Finch's eggs or chicks from the nest. With mixed clutches, they incubate just as reliably, but most of the time do not rear the young of the other birds. The reason for this is probably that the chicks of the other birds, besides

Chestnut-breasted Finches are compatible with other birds and are relatively easy to breed.

A pair of Spice Finches.

"The opinion that estrildid finches foster-bred by Society Finches are always unfit for further breeding, since they allegedly do not incubate correctly or do not rear the young properly, is not always justified. . ."

having a different form, also display widely varying behavior to which the foster-parents do not react.

Foster-parent breeding succeeds at best, of course, with closely related species, but it also has succeeded repeatedly with the small-beaked astrilds, whereby the prerequisite is that the Society Finches become accustomed early enough to accepting animal food. In any case, foster-parent breeding does not succeed all the time. It is especially apt to fail when the other species involved have reared their young a relatively long time with animal food, since the Society Finches after a few days switch to feeding with seeds.

The opinion that estrildid finches foster-bred by Society Finches are always unfit for further breeding, since they allegedly do not incubate correctly or do not rear the young properly, is not always justified, although it is true that a very negative natural selection can result from rearing the offspring of poorly breeding parents. It has also been stated that other estrildid finches

A Chestnut-breasted Finch. Sex differentiation is difficult in this species.

A lovely pair of White-headed Munias.

reared by Society Finches cannot be used for breeding because they have taken on the traits of the Society Finches and would never again breed with a bird of their own species. This opinion is only partially valid, namely when the young birds remain with the foster parents after they have fledged. Having any of the traits of Society Finches passed on to the young birds can be prevented by separating them from the Society Finches immediately after they have fledged; then they are mostly ready to breed with birds of their own species at the proper time.

Most Society Finches are brown, white-yellow and white or piebald, and also in the most varying distribution. There are also, however, Society Finches which have been bred purely one-colored, three-colored, cream-colored, and gray piebald (so-called "tempered," nougat-colored, etc.). There are also powdered Society Finches and such with double top and ruff. Through targeted breeding, the Japanese have developed a number of varieties, white or mainly dark-colored, whereby some types also have feather tops as well as curls and helmet plumes. White Society

Fledged: means that the young bird has grown the feathers necessary for flight.

A pair of Spice Finches. This species can be recommended for beginning breeders, as they are easy to keep and can be kept in an outdoor aviary if, of course, adequate shelter is provided.

A White-backed Bronze Mannikin. This species has a wide distribution and consists of several races.

"Society Finches should be kept in pairs in single cages, since they like to slide over to other birds in a nest and disturb them."

A Hill Bronze Mannikin, *Lonchura kelaarti*. This species is occasionally available to fanciers.

Finches often show eye ailments, which is why they at best should be bred over schizopodas. They are nourished with silver, Senegal, and spray millet, canary seed and sprouts, egg food, ant pupae (especially when they are to be used as foster-parent birds), and soft food and plenty of green food.

Society Finches should be kept in pairs in single cages, since they like to slide over to other birds in a nest and disturb them. Otherwise, they are modest, hardy and quite peaceful birds which are very friendly and easily disposed to begin breeding. In appearance, the sexes cannot be told apart. An infallible identifying sign is the cock's song. The enticing calls of both sexes are, however, different; the cock entices with "oui" "quoi" without an r; the hen

A self-chocolate Society Finch. Society Finches are also known as Bengalese Finches.

An array of Society Finches. These birds have been domesticated for centuries and are highly recommended for beginners.

A crested fawn-and-white Society Finch. Society Finches are often used as foster-parents for the young of other, more unreliable, finch species.

A chestnut-and-white Society Finch. Society Finches are bred in various color and plumage patterns.

A Lavender Waxbill is a peaceful bird that should be given adequate amounts of live food.

"As domesticated birds, the Society Finches have obviously forgotten how to build free-standing nests."

buzzes with a humming r.

The nest is built artistically in a small box. As domesticated birds, the Society Finches have obviously forgotten how to build free-standing nests. The clutch consists of four to seven eggs, the incubation period is four to sixteen days, and the young become fledged in about three weeks. Mixed breeds have been bred with a number of amadines, thick-beaked estrildid finch species, and have partially proven in the male sex to be capable of reproducing, in the female sex mostly not.

The Indian Silverbill, *Euodice malabarica*, is regularly available, but never in large numbers, in the bird trade. From Near India and Ceylon, it has a length of 11-13 cm. Both sexes have the same coloring. This quiet, easy to acclimatize, and

The White-backed Bronze Mannikin is a most likely ancestor of the well-known Society Finch.

The Society Finch does not exist in the wild but is a product of years of hybridization by man.

The female Cut-throated Finch does not possess the tell-tale ribbon of color around the neck.

A Magpie Mannikin.

Northern Brown-backed Blue-billed Mannikin, *Spermestes bicolor nigriceps*, in east Africa from south Somalia to Tanzania and Zambia; and, finally, the Southern Brown-backed Blue-billed Mannikin, *Spermestes bicolor rufodorsalis*, in southeast Africa from Mozambique and south Malawi to Natal and Transvaal. For rearing, flour worms, ant pupae, and egg food are needed.

The Bronze Mannikin, *Spermestes cucullata*, from tropical Africa southwards to Angola, Transvaal, Natal and Transkei, is a reasonably good breeding bird, lively, mobile, steadfast and modest. It exists in only three races which vary only slightly from one another. Its length is 9 cm. In the cage, it shows itself to be aggressive and picks fights even with considerably larger cage

"The Bronze Mannikin . . . is a reasonably good breeding bird, lively, mobile, steadfast and modest."

A pair of Gray-headed Silverbills, *Odontospiza caniceps*. This species is also called the Pearl-headed Silverbill, and it is often classified as *Lonchura caniceps*.

neighbors and wins. Its song is not loud and is unimpressive.

The Bronze Mannikin builds a not very artistic nest in a box with a narrow entry hole. These nests must be attached very firmly to the wall or the bars of the cage, because the nest mound is very flat and has the same height as the entrance hole, so that the eggs can roll out of the nest as the birds fly in or out if the nest is not sufficiently secured and shakes a lot. The cock's courtship dance consists of hopping up and down with continuous turning of the head, as is the case with most of the amadines. The clutch consists of four to seven eggs, which are incubated by both mates of the pair in 12 days. The young leave the nest at an age of about three weeks. When fledged, they must be

Gray-headed Silverbills are often given the species name *griseicapilla*.

"In the cage...[the Bronze Mannikin] shows itself to be aggressive and picks fights even with considerably larger cage neighbors and wins."

The Magpie Mannikin is not readily available in the bird trade although it is a hardy and compatible species.

A pair of Bronze Mannikins. Bronze Mannikins have also been called Bronze-winged Mannikins.

removed from the breeding area, because otherwise they will go to the nest and disturb the parents during another incubation. Mixed breeds have been bred with the Blue-billed Mannikin, the Society Finch, the Indian Silverbill, Magpie Mannikin, Spice Finch, Bib Finch, and the African Silverbill.

"The Cut-throat Finch . . . is one of the larger estrildid finches. It is a strong bird and relatively easy to breed. It is therefore suitable for the novice fancier."

The Cut-throat Finch, *Amadina fasciata*, is one of the estrildid finches that have been imported for a long time and are always readily available in the bird trade. Its extensive distribution area extends from Senegal to Abyssinia and from there throughout east Africa to Transvaal; there are several different races in this area. The Cut-throat Finch is 12-13 cm long; it is one of the larger estrildid finches. It is a strong bird and relatively easy to breed. It is therefore suitable for the novice fancier. The sexes can easily be told apart, as the hen does not have the red crop band and the chestnut-brown spot on the stomach. Its song is quiet, sounding like a ventriloquist, and consists of an unusual humming which is emitted with a stretched neck, ruffled head feathers and bending movements. The enticing call is a sparrow-like "schilp."

Cocks and hens become very unpleasant during the breeding season in that they ransack the nests of other birds in the community cage or in the birdroom, chase off the old birds, throw out the eggs and young, and take the nest-building materials to build their own nests. This bad situation can seldom be corrected, but you should try to dissuade these birds from their lust for other's nests by providing them

A Cut-throat Finch in flight.

Society Finches come in a variety of colors and patterns.

with as much nest-building material as possible. Unfortunately, the hens suffer from egg-laying difficulties. The animals also nest unreliably, at least in the beginning, abandon eggs and young, or throw them out of the nest. The clutch consists of four to nine eggs, the incubation time is 12-13 days; the young leave the nest in the fourth week and are soon fledged.

The youth plumage is the same as the adult plumage, only the colors are generally duller; the cock sometimes does not have the red crop band or the breast spot or both. Cocks bred in captivity always leave the nest with a red neck band and brown breast spot. The Zebra Finch and Cut-throat Finch excel in respect to great fertility. Often four or five incubations occur one after the other. A good breeding pair rears 20-25 young annually. Dr. Karl Russ mentions in his book, *The Foreign Domesticated Birds,* a Cut-throat Finch pair which nested for three years without interruption and incubated and reared a total of 176 young. An amazing performance! Mixed breeds have been bred with the Indian Silverbill, the Society Finch, the Java Sparrow, the Parson Finch and with the closest related species, the Red-headed Finch. The hybrids of the latter crossing, however, proved in the first generation to be fertile only in the male sex; the hybrid hens, however, become fertile again in the second and third generation by reverse breeding.

The Red-headed Finch, *Amadina erythrocephala,* is the closest relative of the Cut-throat Finch and has a length of 14 cm, making it larger

Reverse breeding: a breeding technique which involves breeding a hybrid bird back to one of the parent species in order to achieve fertility in both sexes of the hybrid.

A young Red-headed Finch. Note the lack of coloration on this juvenile.

The Red-headed Finch is closely related to the Cut-throat Finch, but it is a bit larger.

A lovely Gray-headed Silverbill.

than the latter. This bird was imported again in 1954 after a long interruption; it is now readily available. It is distributed in south and west Angola, Namibia and South Africa to west Zimbabwe, Natal and to the Cape area. It resembles the Cut-throat Finch very much, is modest, hardy and easy to breed. There are differing opinions about its compatibility. One side claims that it is compatible, while the other side asserts that is an intolerable troublemaker from which no nest is safe. As is so often the case, it depends on the conditions under which it is kept. However, it is said to be generally quieter than the Cut-throat Finch, but it does show the tendency to inspect the nests of other birds.

Breeding is simple, but the hens (which, by the way, do not have any red head plumage) are very sensitive

Yellow-headed Gouldian Finch. Breeders are now trying to perfect a blue color phase of this species.

". . .[The Red-headed Finch] resembles the Cut-throat Finch very much, is modest, hardy and easy to breed. There are differing opinions about its compatibility."

The Zebra Finch has long served as goodwill ambassador to those entering the world of finches for the first time.

"When the Red-headed Finches fight, they hiss at each other like ganders while moving their necks in a similar manner."

An array of Red-headed Finches. The hens are those birds that lack the red coloration on their heads. Red-headed Finches are very sensitive to disturbances around the nest.

to disturbances at the nest. The nest is built very sloppily, is roofed over, and has a relatively narrow entrance. The Red-headed Finch cocks bred in captivity are said to always leave the nest with red head plumage, while the young cocks in the wild generally have a gray head, sometimes mixed with red feathers. When the Red-headed Finches fight, they hiss at each other like ganders while moving their necks in a similar manner. Mixed breeds have been bred with the Cut-throat Finch. They have the same fertility as the Cut-throat Finch.

A pair of Cut-throat Finches. Cut-throat Finches become unruly during the breeding season, so care must be taken to prevent them from doing too much damage.

SUGGESTED READING

THE COMPLETE BIRDS OF THE WORLD (ILLUSTRATED EDITION)
by Michael Walters
ISBN 0-87666-894-5
TFH H-1022

This book lists every bird species in the world and gives for each the family, range, common and scientific names, and related important data. Birds of 120 different families are shown in beautiful (and mostly large) full-color photos; there are more than 550 full-color illustrations in total. This magnificent volume enables bird watchers, aviculturists, dealers, and scientists to learn the habitat, distribution, feeding and nesting habits, clutch size, incubation, and fledging period of every family of birds in existence. Written by one of the world's foremost avian authorities and illustrated with some of the finest natural history photographs ever published, this immensely colorful and useful book will be referred to for many years, regardless of where in the world the reader may live. The book is fully indexed with both common and scientific names for ease of reference. A treasure to own and a pleasure to show, it is one of the finest ornithological works ever produced.

BIRD DISEASES: An Introduction to the Study of Birds in Health and Disease
by Drs. L. Arnall and I.F. Keymer
ISBN 0-87666-950-X
TFH H-964

This is a highly specialized book written for bird pathologists and dealers. It requires a thorough knowledge of biology to be understood, but experienced bird lovers can recognize symptoms and diseases from the many illustrations and will thus be able to treat their own birds, since "bird doctors" are so few and far between.

FINCHES AND SOFT-BILLED BIRDS
by Henry Bates and Robert Busenbark
ISBN 0-87666-421-4
TFH H-908

The most complete book on seed-eating, soft-billed birds (as opposed to hard-billed or parrot-like birds). Every important cage bird is discussed and illustrated in color. No other book in any language lists so many known pet birds. Used extensively all over the world as an identification guide, this volume is a must for bird reference libraries in pet shops and zoos, general reference libraries, and for governmental agencies concerned with the identification of birds.

THE COMPLETE CAGE AND AVIARY BIRD HANDBOOK
by David Alderton
ISBN 0-86622-113-1
TFH H-1087

Author David Alderton, well known for his books and articles on avicultural subjects, examines the whole field of cage and aviary birds. Treating the species by family, he provides current information on both the popular species and many of the less commonly seen birds as well. Highlighted with black and white photos and 167 full-color photos that help the reader to identify the species and varieties, along with excellently detailed illustrations showing the design of aviaries and furnishings.

INDEX

FINCHES
AND THEIR CARE
TS-107

KEVIN

HarperCollins
PUBLISHERS
200
Since 1817

First published in hardback in Great Britain by
HarperCollins Children's Books in 2017

HarperCollins Children's Books is a division of HarperCollins Publishers Ltd. A CIP catalogue record for this book is available from the British Library.

Visit our website at www.harpercollins.co.uk

ISBN: 978-0-00-820741-0
Printed and bound in China
10 9 8 7 6 5 4 3 2 1

And when it was teatime, invisible Sid…
Well, look to your right and you'll see what he did.

So... Sid scribbled on walls and he scribbled on floors.

He bounced on the beds and he swung from the doors.

He hosed down the dog and he frightened the hens.

He left all the lids off of Kevin's new pens.

Now I have to report, with a slight note of dread,
That Sidney was hatching a plan in his head.
A plan oh so cheeky, so tricksy, so clever...

Invisible Sid = Bestest fun ever!

Are you catching my drift? Do you see what I mean?
You can't get told off if you cannot be seen!

Sid smiled and said, “Hi!” as each one came toward him,
But oddly, the strange-featured creatures ignored him.
Big Red, Little Blue, the one shaped like a kidney,
They nodded to Kev, but they looked straight through Sidney.

CHEZ KEVIN

By the time they had rocked up at Kevin’s front door
The facts of the matter were hard to ignore.
Here in Kev’s world, as I’m sure you are seeing,
’Twas Sidney who was the imaginary being.

They passed lots of beasties
that looked pretty silly.

Some hairy. Some slimy. Some leggy. Some frilly.

"Kevin? You're Kevin!" said Sid with a squeal.
"I cannot believe that you're actually real!
You're just like my drawing! No need to pretend.
We'll play every day. You can be my best friend."
Kevin just smiled and took Sid by the hand,
and they started to walk through this magical land.

When he got to the top, what a sight to behold!
Just look at that sky – what a fine shade of gold.
The tree trunks were purple, the leaves made of jelly.
The flowers were huge and incredibly smelly.
The clouds were all star-shaped, the rainbow was dotty.
The ladybirds stripy, the bumblebees spotty.
The grass was a carpet of mint-green and yellow.
And who's this familiar sort of a fellow?

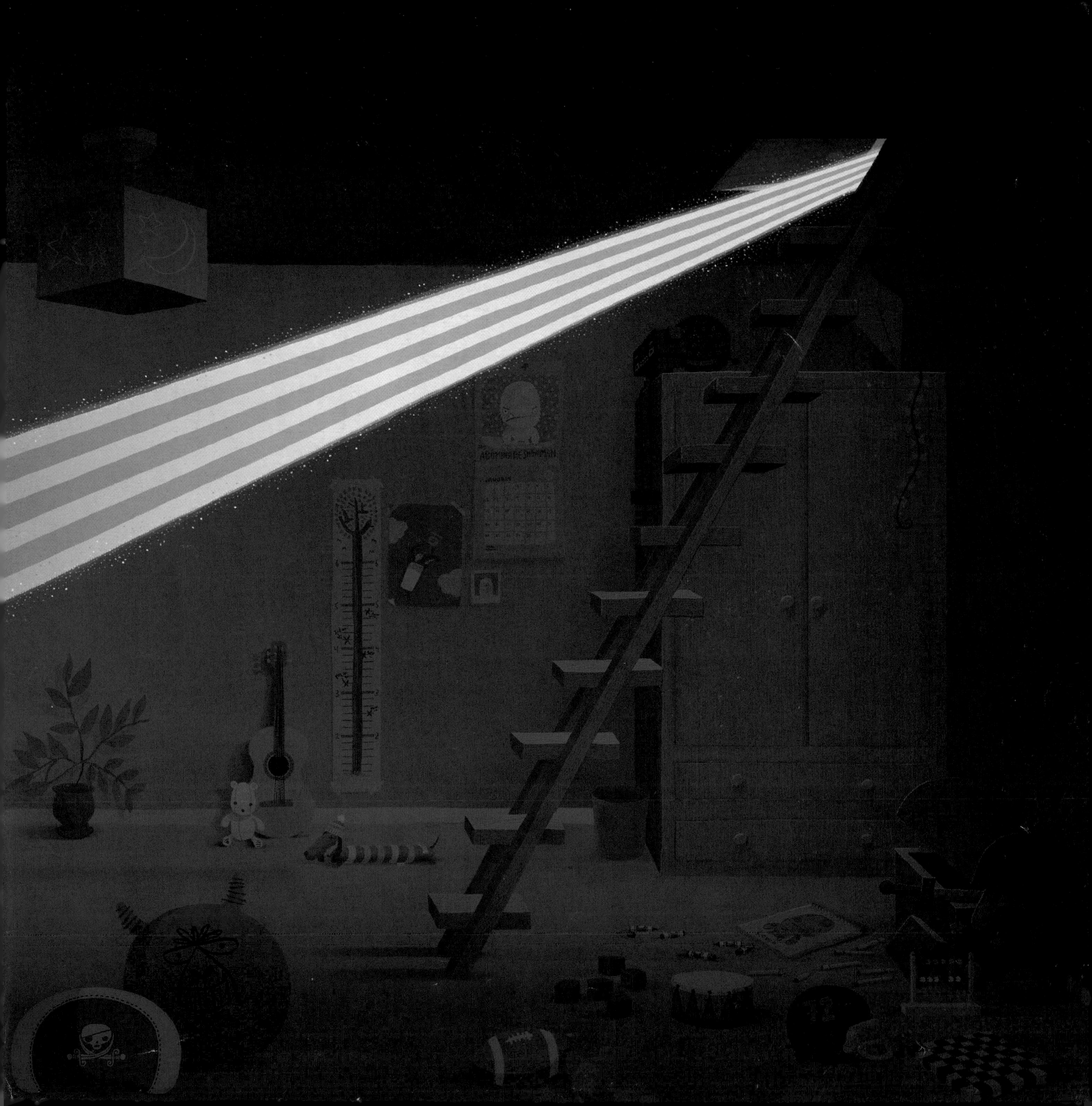

Grumpily Sid made his
way up the stairs
And put on his PJs
(the ones with the bears).

He sat in the darkness,
his mood not improving
When slowly the door
to the hatch started moving.

Suddenly light flooded
in through the chink
Which Sid could have sworn
was vanilla and pink.

Excited and nervous
all at the same time
He took a deep breath
and he started to climb.

"He's kind but he's clumsy
and that, I'm afraid,
Is why he's to blame for
the mess that's been made."

Mum rolled her eyes and her cheeks went bright red.
"That's enough Sidney. Now, please go to bed.
And have a good think 'cos these fibs have to end –
you must not blame *your* mess on a make-believe friend!"

“Um... he’s ever so tall
and he’s ever so wide.
And ever so smiley,”
the little boy lied.

“Has only one tooth.
Is as strong as a gorilla.
Has lots of pink spots
on a fur of vanilla.

“Whenever I’m down
with that sad, lonely feeling
He comes down to stay
through the hatch in my ceiling.

Mum was confused as she looked at the chair.
'Twas quite plain to see there was no Kevin there.
A satisfied Sid simply stood there and smiled.
"Well, what does he looks like?" said Mum to the child.

This isn't the first time
that Sid's been in trouble:

Mum folded her arms as she spoke to the lad.
"Now Sidney, remember the talk that we had?"
But Sid, he was hatching a plan in his head,
And before she could finish the little chap said...

"I didn't do it! I'm Innocent Sid.
But if you'll just listen I'll tell you who did.
Kevin! Y-yes, that's right, Kevin. He did it.
Why don't you just ask him? He'll have to admit it."

And this is the reason they're looking so glum.

(Sid's dinner was up on the table before,
But now it's an upside-down tea-on-the-floor.)

This is Sid Gibbons.

And this is his mum.

For Kitty.
And Cleverin.

Written and illustrated by

HarperCollins *Children's Books*

Just as Kev started to
clean up the floor
In walked his dad
through the wrecked
kitchen door.

Slowly, but surely,
his cheeks went bright red.
"That's enough Kevin,
now please go to bed!"

It was then that Sid noticed as Kevin walked by
A single blue tear welling up in his eye.

Suddenly Sidney did not feel so clever.
He actually felt like the least best-friend ever.
He went up the stairs full of sorrow and guilt
To where he found Kevin tucked under his quilt.

"Kevin," Sid whispered, "Oh, Kevin stop crying.
I've been really selfish, there is no denying.
I'm terribly sorry I've got you in trouble,
I'm going to put right all my wrongs at the double."

So... Sid scrubbed all the walls and he scrubbed all the floors.
He mended the bed and he fixed all the doors.
He brushed down the dog and he settled the hens.
He tidied away all of Kevin's new pens.

And then he gave Kevin a card that he'd made.
"My drawing is not very good I'm afraid.
But I hope that you like it and find in your heart
A way to be friends like we were at the start."

Kevin just smiled and he gave Sid a cuddle,
And there they both stood in a big teardrop puddle.

Kevin showed Sid the way back to the hatch.
They said their goodbyes as Sid unhooked the latch.
But before he went down a reformed Sidney Gibbons
Collected some flowers and tied them with ribbons.

Back in his room Sidney got himself dressed
Then ran down the stairs, flowers clutched to his chest.
He dashed through the house from one room to another.
At last, in the kitchen, our Sid found his mother.

"Mum, I am sorry for causing such trouble.
I am the one turned the birdbath to rubble.
I messed up my room and *I* ruined my pens.
I should not blame it all on my innocent friends."

Then Sidney gave her the beautiful posy,
And Mum was so happy her cheeks went all rosy.

Now, this is Sid Gibbons.

And this is his mum.

And there on the slide's our invisible chum.

Since Sid learned his lesson
and stopped blaming others
Kevin and him have been
closer than brothers.

I wonder if you have a make-believe friend.
An invisible pal upon whom you depend.
If no-one believes you don't grumble or moan,
'Cos one thing's for certain...

...You're not on your own.

CHOPPER

COFFEE